From Brooklyn to the Olympics

From Brooklyn to the Olympics

The Hall of Fame Career of Auburn University Track Coach Mel Rosen

———

CRAIG DARCH

FOREWORD BY HARVEY GLANCE

NewSouth Books

Montgomery

NewSouth Books
105 S. Court Street
Montgomery, AL 36104

Library of Congress Cataloging-in-Publication Data

Darch, Craig.
From Brooklyn to the Olympics : The Hall of Fame Career of Auburn University
track coach Mel Rosen / Craig Darch.
pages cm
Includes bibliographical references.
ISBN 978-1-58838-305-1 (hardcover) — ISBN 978-1-60306-346-3 (ebook)
1. Rosen, Mel, 1928- 2. Track and field coaches—United States—Biography.
3. Auburn University—Track and field—History. I. Title.
GV697.R626D33 2014
796.42092—dc23
[B]

2013045899

Design by Randall Williams

Printed in the United States of America
by Maple Press

*On page ii: Rosen in his office in the Auburn University Athletics Department.
During track season Rosen still spends each day calling old friends and preparing for
practice (Eric O. Darch).*

*On the jacket: Front, Mel Rosen at the 1990 Goodwill Games after the 200 meter
race. From background to foreground, Róbson da Silva of Brazil, Michael Johnson,
and Dennis Mitchell (David Tulis). Back, Rosen at the Hutsell-Rosen track (Auburn
University Photographic Services, Rosen collection).*

*Unless otherwise noted, all photos in this book are used courtesy of Mel Rosen from
his personal files.*

To

My wife Gabi,
who leads by example

My son Eric,
who is a mensch

Wilbur Darch,
May his memory be for a blessing.

CONTENTS

FOREWORD

HARVEY GLANCE

I first met Coach Rosen in 1975 when he was recruiting me for Auburn's track and field team. When he visited me and my family in Phenix City, Alabama, I liked him immediately. So did my mom and dad. I hadn't met many people with a New York accent back then. But no matter the accent, I saw right away he was sincere, honest, funny, and respectful. But most of all I saw that he was a competitor. He wanted to win and knew how to train athletes to get the very best out of them.

Coach Rosen told me on one of his visits to my home that I could count on him to be at the track every day and be by my side. He was true to his word. It didn't matter whether it was a practice, a conference meet, an international competition, or the Olympics, Coach Rosen was by my side helping me and the team do our best to win. Coach Rosen treated all team members the same. If I came to practice late, I would hear about it from him. There was never a hint of favoritism. We respected Coach Rosen and did everything we could do to run our best for him. We knew he was the real deal.

He didn't just teach us running technique, he taught us life lessons. When you ran for Coach Rosen, you felt you were part of a team. What made Coach Rosen a world-class coach and an even better person? Read Craig Darch's biography on Mel Rosen, and you will find out how a Jewish kid from Brooklyn came to Auburn and became an iconic coach. It is a great story, and I am glad it's being told! I am grateful Coach Rosen played such a big part in my life. War Eagle!

PREFACE

My interest in writing the Mel Rosen story had its roots in South Bend, Indiana, where I grew up. My father, an avid sports fan, always talked about Jewish athletes. In his mind, if an athlete was Jewish, then his or her achievement was even more noteworthy, something to talk about and, as Jews, something to be proud of, because American Jews are always looking for Jewish sports heroes.

In high school I was a high jumper and had moderate success; I once cleared 6'1" in a conference meet—not too bad an achievement for the mid-1960s. I followed with interest the 1960 and 1964 Olympic competition between John Thomas, the first U.S. high jumper to clear seven feet, and his bitter Russian rival, the great Valeriy Brumel, who beat him in both Olympic games. My interest in track continued during graduate school at the University of Oregon, then the epicenter of United States collegiate track and field. It was a great place to be if you enjoyed the sport. Eugene, Oregon, has been home to world-class athletes like Alberto Salazar to thousands of amateurs who run for the mere enjoyment. I often attended meets at the historic Hayward Field, named after Bill Hayward, Oregon's first track and field coach from 1904–47.

I arrived in Auburn in the summer of 1982 to take a position as an assistant professor in special education. Over the ensuing years I got to know Mel Rosen, then the head track and field coach, by following Auburn track, running into him around town, often at the public library, as well as talking to him at our local synagogue. We sometimes talked about his early years growing up in Brighton Beach, where he played sports with his friends and spent summer hours on the beach. As I got to know Mel better, I became intrigued with his story. How does a Brooklyn Jewish kid, raised during the Great Depression, become head track and field coach at Auburn, a quintessential Southern university, and then wind up as a 1992 Olympic head coach? It seemed to me that such a journey, one that included coaching during the turbulent civil rights struggles and the Vietnam era protests of the 1960s would be well worth researching and telling.

To prepare for writing, I read books from several areas: sports, Jewish history, immigration to the United States, and civil rights struggles in the South. I also studied newspaper accounts, memorabilia, and photographs that documented Rosen's professional achievements and his personal life. Two Auburn University athletic directors and several other athletic department administrators talked with me about Auburn track and field under Rosen's guidance. I interviewed his former athletes and fellow coaches. Finally, I interviewed several athletes from the 1992 Barcelona Olympic Games.

Rosen provided letters he had received over the years from friends, family, athletes, and colleagues. He also made available to me files he had gathered for some 50 years. It was a treat to meet him in his office and look through his papers. There was an enormous amount of information. Rosen, like his predecessor Wilbur Hutsell, kept copious records and filed most of them.

My wife and I made two trips to Brooklyn as part of my research. We walked Rosen's former neighborhood and saw two apartment houses where he lived with his mother during his school years. One of the apartments was where Mrs. Weinstock, his landlady, introduced the young Mel to gambling. We also walked to the former location of Chaim's Pool Hall, a hangout for Rosen and his friends; it is now a Russian Bakery. We visited Abraham Lincoln High School where Rosen starred as a middle-distance runner, as well as the special collections room of the Brooklyn Public Library. Our visits provided some of the backdrop for this book: Brighton Beach, once a Jewish enclave in the 1930s and '40s, is now home to Hispanic and Russian immigrants. Additional background information was obtained in visits to the archives and special collections departments of the University of Iowa and Auburn University.

Most importantly, this book relies on the memories of Mel Rosen himself, as well as recollections of his family, his Brighton Beach school buddies and other friends he has made along the way. In all, I interviewed 40 people for this book, several of them multiple times. The gracious input from all of these people helped me write an intimate, anecdote-rich portrait of Mel, a man who achieved excellence both as a person and a coach during his long, richly layered life.

Once I decided to write Rosen's story, I began to experience the writer's fear that I might not be able to do justice to his many accomplishments, his larger-than-life persona. As always, I turned to my wife, Gabi, and expressed my self-doubts. And as usual, she gave me advice that helped me get started on this work.

She told me she had just finished reading a book by Anne Lamott. In the book, Lamott tells a story about her younger brother, about 12 years old at the time, who was assigned to write a report on birds. Her brother was frozen with self-doubt and could not force himself to begin his writing assignment. The length and complexity of the task overwhelmed him. After several weeks of procrastination marked by many anxious moments, and with the due date fast approaching, in utter desperation he went to his father and asked how he should begin working on such a complicated assignment. John Lamott sat for a few moments and said nothing then put his arm around his son and said in a kind, but matter-of-fact way, "Bird by bird, buddy. Just take it bird by bird."[1]

I took my wife's and Lamott's advice, so here it is, the Mel Rosen story told as best I could, "bird by bird."

ACKNOWLEDGMENTS

I could not have written this book without the help and support of many people. First, I want to thank NewSouth Books: Suzanne La Rosa, publisher, and Randall Williams, editor extraordinaire, for accepting the Mel Rosen story. My thanks also goes to Dr. Jay Gogue for believing in the book. I spent considerable time in Auburn's archives for the last few years. Their collection of Auburn sports documents is impressive. Even more impressive are Dwayne Cox, head of Special Collection and Archives, and Greg Schmidt and John Varner. Each always made sure I found the documents I was looking for. Mel Rosen's family opened up their lives, by telling their stories and helping add a rich flavor to the book. Mel's wife Joan was always eager to discuss their long, love-filled journey together.

Mel's daughters Karen and Laurie spoke freely about the role their father played in their lives. Their enthusiasm and sharp insights made the book better. I want to thank David Housel, Auburn's former athletic director and foremost authority on Auburn sports history, for reading and commenting on the manuscript. Thanks also to Brian Keeter for reading the manuscript. Coach Pat Dye was gracious enough to talk to me at length about Rosen's track and field program. Jon Waggoner got behind the book and kept the process moving with his wise counsel, humor, and lawyer's eye for detail. Tyler Adams helped me in the final stages of publication. And Joel Sanders of Montgomery read the galleys and made numerous valuable suggestions.

Friends played an important role in completing this work. Mike Friedman and Henry Stern contributed their recollections of Auburn Jewish history. Mike Halperin was a constant source of encouragement and friendship; there is no better friend. Thanks also to my many interviewees, especially Kenny Howard, Auburn's former trainer; Buddy Davidson, former assistant athletic director; Jerry Smith, track star and Mel's assistant coach for several years; and Harvey Glance, who spoke with me twice about his relationship with his mentor and coach, Mel Rosen.

I want to thank my mother, Dorothy, who never let a week go by without asking about the book. She is an amazing woman who is an inspiration to my entire family. My sister Debbie, the spirit of our family, asked questions that helped me sharpen my thinking and writing. My brother Lance, a poet in words and heart, was a driving force in helping me complete the writing. My brother Mike, now the patriarch of the family, took interest in the project from day one and offered his encouragement throughout the long process of getting this work published. I will always be indebted to them. Most importantly, I want to thank my son, Eric, and my wife, Gabi. Eric took photographs, helped me keep computer and paper files organized, and listened to and read the manuscript. His love and support made it possible to complete this book. Finally, Gabi, my wife of over 40 years, has been there from the beginning. She read and edited every page of the manuscript, listened to me when my confidence waned, and put her arm around me and guided me back on the right path. She is my partner and the love of my life.

From Brooklyn to the Olympics

I

THE PROMISE FULFILLED

(1928–45)

"It never occurred to me that because my father died when I was young it would be harder for me. Maybe because my mother made sure I had everything I needed."

We are a country of immigrants; 26 million came to the United States between 1880 and 1924, the period of the third and largest of the four great migrations to our shores. Our story as Americans is rooted in the lives and circumstances of our ancestors who risked everything to make the difficult journey across the Atlantic to Ellis Island and other ports of entry. More than two million of that third wave of immigrants were Jewish and of those, 75 percent were from Russia.[1] Why did they come? Irving Howe, one of the great chroniclers of Jewish immigration to the United States answers this way: "The main reason was to get away. To get away from the czar and his army. To get away from the stagnation, the hunger, the hopelessness that Jews faced in Russia and other eastern European countries."[2] It was to give their children opportunities that were unavailable in their countries of origin. Jews were lured to America by "tales of wondrous opportunity and by the advent of cheap trans-Atlantic fares."[3]

Thus, the Mel Rosen story in some ways begins on a cloudy, cold March 1, 1881, in St. Petersburg, Russia. On that fateful day, Alexander II, considered a tolerant ruler by Russian Jews because of his moderate liberalism, was assassinated by a member of a revolutionary organization, the *Narodnaya Volya* (People's Will).[4] Alexander II's relatively moderate reign came to an abrupt end, and power shifted to the repressive and anti-Semitic Alexander

3

III. In the aftermath, the lives of several million Eastern European Jews changed drastically. Almost immediately after the assassination, a wave of pogroms—state-sponsored killing of Jews and the looting of their property—swept across Russia and the Ukraine in response to a rumor that Jews had assassinated Alexander II. Hundreds of Jews were murdered, thousands more injured, and countless others driven from their homes in *shtetls* (small towns and hamlets) throughout the Russian empire.[5] In Howe's words, the 1881 pogroms left the Jews "stunned and bleeding."[6] New anti-Semitic legislation, called the May Laws of 1882, "undid the modest gains won during the early years of Alexander II's reign and severely curtailed Jewish residency, occupational, and educational rights." The May Laws prohibited Jews from buying property in rural areas, banned Jews from doing business on Sundays and Christian holidays, and prohibited new Jewish settlements. Historian S. M. Dubnow termed the May Laws "legislative pogroms."[7] The aim of these measures was the destruction of the Jewish community in Russia. These violent circumstances, along with a series of repressive laws limiting the occupations Jews could pursue and the institution of quotas for secondary and university education, precipitated a massive emigration of Russian Jewry to the United States, Canada, and England.

ROSEN'S GRANDPARENTS ON BOTH sides were among the approximately 200,000 Jews who fled a second wave of bloody pogroms during 1903–06. Odessa and its surrounding *shtetlach* were prime targets for anti-Jewish violence. Likely his mother's family, the Kaminskys, who were from that area, saw the death and destruction of the pogroms. Like other immigrants before them, they fled to the United States for the promise of a better life for themselves and their children. However, instead of finding "streets paved with gold," they found poverty and struggle, often in the form of densely populated tenements on New York's Lower East Side, a ghetto filled with repressive sweat shops and the grind of long work days. The New York State Bureau of Labor Statistics put it this way in a turn of the century economic report: "The very best workers could earn $10 per week. Some even with the aid of their families and working 14 hours a day could earn only $12 to $15 per week."[8] Like most of the other Jewish immigrants of that period,

Rosen's parents and grandparents probably came to Ellis Island with little more than the clothes they wore and what few possessions they could carry.

The details of Rosen's paternal grandparents' journey to America have been forgotten, but we do know his mother, Mollie Kaminsky, came to the United States in 1906, at the age of 14; she was the oldest girl of five boys and five girls. Her family had made a meager living farming. How they were able to fund and orchestrate their escape to America while so many others remained behind, we don't know. In any case, Mollie, her parents, and her nine brothers and sisters did escape their hometown near the port city of Odessa.

Rosen remembers some of his mother's tales about Odessa. "Mama had vivid recollections of Odessa. She told me visiting Odessa with her father was a favorite activity for her. She loved the city because of how beautifully dressed some of the women were. She also told me it could be a dangerous place." The great Russian writer Isaac Babel provides a portrait that helps us understand how a young girl like Mollie might be taken in by the city. "In Odessa, there are sweet and relaxing spring evenings, the strong scent of acacias, and, over the dark sea, a moon which radiates a steady, irresistible light."[9] Historian Steven Zipperstein writes that in Yiddish folklore Odessa came to be associated with indifference to religion, a criminal underworld, and glamorous women. Odessa was considered a city like no other in Russia. Odessa was also known as a "hot bed of ethnic, religious, and economic rivalries."[10] Mollie's indifference to many of the rituals of Judaism may have had its beginnings in her visits to Odessa as a girl.

While we have no account passed down from Mollie Kaminsky or others in her family of their voyage, it was likely difficult and long; probably two to three weeks on the ship. The trip across the Atlantic was not easy for anyone, but it was particularly hard for those who rode steerage as the Kaminsky family most likely did.

The American philosopher Morris Raphael Cohen, who emigrated from Minsk, Russia, at about the same time as Rosen's mother, describes his family's voyage. "We huddled together in the steerage, literally like cattle—my mother, my sister, and I sleeping in the middle tier, people being above us and below us. . . . We could not eat the food of the ship since it was not kosher. We only asked for hot water into which my mother put a little brandy and sugar to give it a taste."[11]

AFTER ARRIVING AT Ellis Island and successfully making it through the numerous medical examinations, including the feared eye exam, which was often used by authorities to deny entry to the United States, Mollie Kaminsky and her family traveled to Connecticut to begin their new lives. Again, we have no reliable information why they chose Connecticut; one reason may have been that Mollie's father wanted to continue farming, as it was what he knew best. A second reason was that a family member or *landsmanshaftn*, someone from their town near Odessa, had already migrated to Connecticut and invited them to come and begin their new life. Not every Jewish immigrant from Russia was interested in a crowded and loud urban setting. Historian Uri Herscher writes that approximately 3,000 Jewish farmers settled in Connecticut, New Jersey, and upstate New York during this time. Many of these farming ventures were sponsored by Jewish philanthropic groups such as the Hebrew Immigrant Society and the Baron De Hirsh Fund.[12] These organizations purchased large tracts of land and provided low-interest loans to help Jewish farmers settle into rural communities. It's possible the newly arrived Kaminsky family took advantage of this opportunity and settled on a farm in Connecticut. Unfortunately many of these farming ventures were short-lived failures due to unfavorable weather, poor land, and other problems.[13]

Despite offers of low-interest loans to locate in rural communities, most Jews were drawn to New York's Lower East Side with its thriving garment district and array of jobs. Thus, life for Jewish families in rural areas was most likely lonely due to the small number of Jews who elected to settle there.[14] It was probably no different for the recently arrived Kaminsky family.

Life for a Jewish girl in Russia at the turn of the century was not an easy one. Formal education was typically not available to Jewish girls.[15] Girls were expected to help their mothers with household duties until they married and had families of their own. In America, Mollie, being the oldest girl in the family, was still expected to care for her brothers and sisters. As a consequence, Mollie never attended school as a young girl and thus didn't learn to read or write in her native language, which she always regretted. She felt stigmatized by her inability to read and write, and it caused her considerable discomfort. Years later, as an adult, she taught herself to read and write in English. In spite of her own lack of formal schooling, like many immigrants of this time, Mollie knew that an education was a sure ticket to assimilation and upward mobility. Howe and Kenneth Libo captured this drive for learning: "In thousands of Yiddish-speaking homes the word *lernin* (to learn) was spoken with tones of reverence. Enormous sacrifices were made to send children to high school and college."[16] The fervor for education drove the sons and daughters of Jewish immigrants to attend schools at all levels. In fact, as Henry Feingold points out, an increasingly large number of children in Jewish neighborhoods graduated from high school, and by the 1930s, high school graduation was the norm.[17]

In 1920, when Mollie was 28, her father died unexpectedly. His death precipitated Mollie's mother's decision to move the entire family from rural Connecticut to New York City, for better employment and marriage opportunities. Family survival required everyone to pitch in. Like most children who came to America as adolescents at the turn of the century, the Kaminsky children were expected to enter the work force as quickly as possible to help support the family.

MOLLIE KAMINSKY MARRIED RATHER late in life; she was 36 when she met and after a brief courtship married Leo Rosen, a Jew who had come to the United States from Prussia. They likely met at a union meeting, as both worked in the garment industry. In the 1930s the garment unions provided not only representation for better wages and working conditions but also social activities for their members and thus fertile ground to meet prospective mates. Leo, who was 48 years old, brought to the marriage a relatively large three-bedroom apartment in the Bronx, as well as a son, Harold, and a daughter, Ethel, from a previous marriage. Melvin Rosen was born the next year, on March 24, 1928, in Tremont Sanitorium.

Leo and Mollie had a happy marriage; they were well-matched. Mollie was spirited, high strung—prone to occasional displays of temper. Leo was even-keeled, stable, and tried to keep things calm in the house. Rosen

Leo & Mollie Rosen, Coney Island, 1934.

describes the balance of personalities: "Every time I did something wrong, which happened with some frequency, my mother would chase me around the dining room table, but my dad always quieted things down. I consider him responsible a number of times for saving my life!"

The family's three-bedroom apartment on Tremont Avenue was considerable space for a family of five during the Great Depression. Rosen remembers his father as a kind man, who was employed in a hat factory in the garment district and made a good living—with a reputation as trustworthy, hard working, and very capable—as he rose to the position of factory foreman. Leo Rosen earned enough as a foreman to support a wife and three children comfortably. He took the Inter-Borough Transit train to work six days a week. He worked 12 hours a day and earned approximately $3,000 a year, considered a good salary in the 1930s, a decade of great anxiety and change. Leo was one of the lucky ones with steady, well-paid employment; New York City in the early 1930s had an unemployment rate of 25 to 30 percent.[18]

When Mel turned three, the Rosen family moved to another three-bedroom apartment, on First Place in Brighton Beach, in a building that still stands. Subsequently the Rosens moved each year to a different apartment in the same building. Rosen recalls that when their apartment needed a fresh coat of paint or repairs they would just pack their belongings and move into another apartment in the same building. So, from an early age, he learned to accept and adapt to frequent changes.

The Rosens' apartment building was only a block and a half from the beach and the boardwalk, a terrific place for a rambunctious boy to romp. Brighton Beach provided a supportive, predominantly Jewish immigrant neighborhood; the vibrant, ethnic community was dubbed "Little Odessa."[19] It was a community bonded by language, traditions, and customs. It was also colorful. An array of ice cream parlors, delis, grocery stores, and secondhand clothing and furniture stores lined Brighton Beach Avenue that stretched along the shore.

Brooklyn hosted an exceptional number of creative people. Writers such as Alfred Kazin and Daniel Fuchs, whose works colorfully describe Brooklyn in the 1930s and '40s, were popular. This was the era of thriving Yiddish theaters such as the Thalia and the Grand.[20] Attending their productions was popular with Jewish immigrants like Mollie. Yiddish plays were filled with adoration of the *Yiddische* mama, the stereotypical Jewish mother. Most plays had a wedding and a happy ending. In addition to writers, actors, artists, and scientists, "Brooklyn spawned some of the most violent and vicious criminals."[21] Dutch Schultz and Abe Reles, well-known Jewish mobsters, controlled illegal gambling operations throughout Brooklyn and Manhattan.

In the 1930s, Yiddish was the language heard on the streets and in the small shops in Brighton Beach and Coney Island, many owned and operated by first-generation Jews set on pursuing the American dream. While the English-language newspaper the *Brooklyn Eagle* (1841–1955), was the most widely read paper in Brooklyn,[22] the Yiddish newspapers, the *Forwertz* and the *Morgan Zurnal*, each costing three cents, were the papers of choice among the borough's Eastern European Jews. Mollie and Leo Rosen spoke Yiddish in their home, and Mel began his life learning English and Yiddish. "Whenever my mother or father didn't want me to understand what they were talking about they spoke to each other in Yiddish. Like my friends, I didn't have an interest in Yiddish. It represented the past to me."

The Rosen family was not religious and thus did not regularly attend any of the numerous, predominantly Orthodox synagogues located in Brighton Beach and Coney Island. While the Rosens did celebrate a few of the Jewish holidays, and sometimes lighted candles Friday nights to observe the Sabbath, and kept kosher—that is, followed the Jewish dietary laws—neither Mel's religious training nor the time he devoted to learning Hebrew left a significant mark on him. "My parents didn't push it. They were ambivalent about attending synagogue themselves. I just wasn't interested at that time in my life. I had a Jewish identity but not a religious one." Like many Jewish boys his age, he preferred other activities than sitting for long, tedious hours in Hebrew School with the rabbi. The Rosens, as assimilated Jews have always done, practiced their faith selectively and ran a mostly secular household. Rosen recalls his father as a quiet person who was not concerned with religion and did not argue about his son's lack of interest in Judaism or push him to attend synagogue. Any friction Mel may have had with his mother about not attending synagogue was typically smoothed over by his father.

Mel entered grammar school in 1933 at age six and attended PS 100 in Brighton Beach through the eighth grade. The student body was predominantly Jewish. It was an excellent school with dedicated, demanding teachers who had high expectations for their students. He lived just across the street from the school and its popular playground. From the beginning, Mel was a good student who rarely missed a day. Because he was a fast learner, his first-grade teacher recommended that Mel skip second grade and pass directly into third. This decision had immediate effects; he now played sports with others who were one year older. While he had usually been the fastest runner on the playground in his grade, now he might not be. But Rosen, ever the optimist, considers skipping second grade an advantage: "I was too good for kids my age so I got into the habit of playing against older kids. While I wasn't the best in this group, I learned how to compete against older, better athletes. It made an impression on me that with hard work I could overcome a lot of things. It helped me to develop mental toughness."

While grammar schools in Brooklyn in the 1930s provided some organized sporting activities, youngsters could also participate in an array of community sports organizations that offered structured athletic competitions. The citywide Public School Athletic League (PSAL), established in 1903, sponsored New York City Public Schools teams in several sports. The Policeman's Athletic League (PAL) also fielded teams in many sports, including track. PAL was founded in 1914 by Captain John Sweeney, the commanding officer of a Lower East Side police precinct. PAL's goal was to keep young people in low-income neighborhoods out of trouble by channeling their energy into recreational and athletic programs. PAL was a wide-ranging program providing parks to play in, arts and crafts activities, and sports, including the first city-sponsored girls basketball league. PAL also sponsored open track meets on weekends. Young athletes like Mel competed without any school affiliation.

These public institutions were a great support for poor families that wanted their children in structured, adult-supervised activities that did not cost anything. Because these sporting events were well organized, the young athletes learned to listen to directions, work with a coach, and be disciplined enough to attend practices regularly. Rosen recalls the Public School Athletic League fondly and recognizes the role it played in his development as an athlete: "From an early age I competed against outstanding kids from around the city. It was good preparation for my high school and college running."

Youngsters also were provided sports activities through organizations like Jewish Community Centers, which were found in Brighton Beach, Coney Island, and throughout Brooklyn.[23] The rivalries between the different ethnic neighborhood teams were a central part of Brooklyn athletic competitions. It was not as simple as one team competing against another. It was the Jews against the Italians, the Irish against the blacks. Fights occurred with some frequency, and Mel used his natural speed to his advantage and ran away to avoid confrontation.

WHEN MEL TURNED SEVEN in 1935, tragedy struck the Rosen family. Leo Rosen collapsed and died of a heart attack at the age of 57. Leo was always an exacting and demanding foreman at the hat factory; his was an Old World work ethic. Leo felt it was a matter of honor and pride to always do your very best on the job. He expected his workers to exert as much effort as he did each day and had little tolerance for slackers. On the day of Leo's death he had confronted several workers who were not adequately performing their assigned duties. A heated argument erupted in Yiddish, and after several minutes of argument Leo collapsed and died. It was a terrible blow to the family. To make matters even worse, soon after, Mel's stepbrother and stepsister, both employed and contributing to the family income, left the home to strike out on their own. While Mel had been close to both, especially Ethel, Mollie had never established a close relationship with either stepchild. Consequently, two sources of income disappeared. "Once my father died money was hard to come by. He didn't leave a will or any money for my mother and me. Our circumstances changed abruptly."

The economic consequences of these events on Mollie and young Mel were immediate. First, she had to find a job again. Through the help of her brother, Louis, who was in the dress business, Mollie found employment working as a "finisher" in a dress factory at a salary of $12 a week, much less than Leo had been earning. A finisher was the woman who trimmed excess thread from the hem of the dress once the sections of the garment were sewn together. This was hot, tiring, and demanding work. "My mother just got up early every morning and went to work, never complaining. She had a job to do and just did it. My mother worked hard her whole life."

That Mollie found employment in the garment district was not surprising, as the clothing industry dominated the city's employment structure for Jewish immigrants, especially women. The garment industry was for decades a source of jobs for Jews and was one option immigrant Jews had during the Depression years[24] when finding other employment was particularly difficult. Help-wanted ads of the period, even in mainstream newspapers including the *New York Times*, used terms like "Christian only," "restricted," and "selected clientele."[25]

Mollie joined the International Ladies' Garment Workers Union (IL-GWU). This and other garment unions such as the International Workers Organization and the Amalgamated Clothing Workers Union brought their members dignity and security.[26] The ILGWU leadership was politically left-wing, often with communist leanings. Mollie, who voted for Democratic candidates, was neither an activist nor particularly political. Rather than political expression, what Mollie gained from the ILGWU was friendship and

The apartment house at 3042 Brighton First Street where seven-year-old Mel moved with his mother, and where the landlady introduced him to gambling (photo by Gabriele Glass Darch).

support in the form of better working conditions and slightly higher wages. Mollie retained her Jewish working-class values and was a pragmatic woman with no use for pretensions or pretentious persons. Mel, like many second-generation Jews growing up in Brooklyn, would develop progressive political views. These attitudes would help him, as we shall see, relate to his diverse group of athletes and coaches over his long career.

Because Mollie worked 12 hours a day in the dress factory, Mel was often left alone to spend his time as he liked, to make his own decisions. These circumstances made him more assertive and more willing to take risks. Thus at an early age, he was especially independent in his thinking. As a result of their new economic hardships, Mollie was also forced to move into a one-room apartment for $20 a month. Four other families rented rooms in the building, and all shared the kitchen and one bathroom located on the first floor of the building. The limited space often led to squabbles between the women while they were cooking. "Eating wasn't much fun. You ate fast and left as soon as possible to make room for others." Their new living arrangement was spartan and required a considerable adjustment for Mollie and Mel. "There was no extra space. I slept on one side of the room and my mother slept on the other side."

Mrs. Weinstock, a crusty, 70-year-old widow, was the landlady. She

Right: 10-year-old Mel, in 1938, already looking off into the distance as if planning his "escape from Brooklyn." Below: Mel's PS 100 Grammar School class. For the 13-year-old, track was already a big part of his life. He is the boy wearing running shoes, third from right.

PUBLIC SCHOOL
100
CLASS 9B3 OF
JUNE 1941

and Mel, despite the age difference, got along famously, and it was Mrs. Weinstock who introduced him at the tender age of 10 to gambling. Each day she would consult with her newfound friend and bet on baseball games and play the numbers. Mel's gambling activities with Mrs. Weinstock lasted for several years. Each week they placed their wagers and waited anxiously for the outcome. Mel's nascent interest in gambling, a common activity among Brooklyn boys during these times, took hold and would continue through his sophomore year in college at Iowa.

As ROSEN APPROACHED HIS twelfth birthday, Mollie expected him to begin studying for his bar mitzvah, a Jewish rite of passage that occurs on a boy's thirteenth birthday and marks the symbolic transition from boyhood to manhood. Added to his already busy schedule of school and organized sports were weekly study sessions with the rabbi to learn Hebrew and study the Torah, the Five Books of Moses. "It's accurate to say I wasn't thrilled with the study sessions with the rabbi. I was interested in other things." This was the first time in young Mel's life that religion played an overt, central role. The year of studying culminated in his bar mitzvah held in a temple in Coney Island. It was a grand affair as all nine of Mel's aunts and uncles as well as cousins and family friends attended and listened to him read from the Torah. Rosen remembers his reading of the Hebrew as adequate, good enough to make the ceremony a success. However, as happens to many assimilated Jewish children, once he completed his bar mitzvah studies, Mel dropped out of Hebrew school and didn't step foot into a synagogue except occasionally for a few of the Jewish holidays.

For second-generation Jewish children of the 1930s and '40s, breaking from the religious, cultural, and language traditions their parents brought from Eastern Europe was an important aspect of creating their own identities and fitting into American society. "As a young boy I was more interested in playing sports, hanging out with the gang. It was the same with most of my friends. We were Americans. I didn't want to hear about the old country."

Mel's Jewish identity, like that of many of his friends, was cultural, not religious. Most of his friends were Jews from the neighborhood. Herb Leber, one of Rosen's childhood friends, remembers Brighton Beach as a

Jewish ghetto: "Growing up it was just Jews. All of us knew there were other types of people but we didn't have much contact with them until we entered Lincoln High School. We lived in an insular community to some extent." The writer Grace Paley, raised in Brooklyn in the 1930s, said she "grew up feeling very sorry for Christians. My idea was there were very few of them in the world."[27]

The importance of a good education was often a topic of conversation between immigrant parents and their children in many Jewish homes in the 1930s and 19's.[28] It was no different in the Rosen home. Mollie took young Mel's schooling seriously and expected him to take advantage of his educational opportunities, which she never had. "Because my mother never attended school and didn't learn to read or write until later in life she always expected me to excel in school. She made it clear that I was to get a good education; that I should take advantage of the sacrifices her mother and father made in coming to America."

DESPITE THE FINANCIAL HARD times, the 1930s were an innocent and uncomplicated time for Mel and his friends. "Brooklyn in the 1930s and 1940s was different. Who had time to get into trouble with so much to do each day?" Sometimes, Mel and his friends would walk the entire five-mile length of the boardwalk to visit Coney Island, a neighborhood bordering Brighton Beach. In Coney Island, the boys would buy hotdogs at Nathan's and spend hours arguing over which baseball team was better, the Brooklyn Dodgers or Mel's favorite, the Saint Louis Browns. Nathan's was well-known throughout New York. For 25 cents Mel would purchase a hot dog and ice cream soda. Notable personalities such as Jimmy Durante, Eddie Cantor, and Cary Grant were regular customers.

Located in Brooklyn were various programs for children, particularly for those from low-income homes. When Mel was 13 he joined the Knothole Club, an organization that provided free tickets and outings to Brooklyn Dodgers baseball games. "The Knothole Club was a great deal. All you had to do was sign up, and they provided free tickets to Dodgers games. We would go as a group, 15 or 20 of us, and all sit in the bleachers. Our favorite player was a Jewish guy, an outfielder, Goody Rosen. We also liked to watch Pee Wee Reese and Pete Reiser." Rosen also attended a summer camp for underprivileged children. As part of a larger trend of assimilation, this represented a concerted effort to provide to young Jewish children not just academic pursuits, but opportunities for games in the outdoors.

While Mel was interested in all sports, he excelled in track; he had been winning local PAL meets in the 50- and 60-yard dashes since he was age nine. These fiercely competitive weekly track meets allowed young athletes to run against others from the New York metropolitan area and helped Rosen develop confidence to compete against anyone.

Mel's early successes in track were transforming. At a young age, he began to see himself as an athlete, an image that was not prevalent among PS 100's Jewish students, who focused more on academics. He liked everything about track. He loved the workouts, the competition against athletes from various parts of the city, and the camaraderie he developed with his teammates. It was at this time that Mel began to think about running track in high school and college. These exhilarating thoughts fueled his desire to compete and gave him a sense of purpose many youngsters his age didn't have. Sport was important to Mel in one other way; the relationships he developed with coaches and teammates filled the void in his life after his father died. "PAL meant a lot to me," Rosen remembers. "It gave me male authority figures, something I didn't have at home. Our coaches were all volunteers and I looked up to them." That pattern persisted; through the years, Rosen would develop his closest male relationships with coaches and, later, his coaching colleagues.

MEL ENTERED ABRAHAM LINCOLN High School in 1941 at the age of 13, one to two years younger than most of his classmates. He brought to Lincoln a well-established, competitive nature and quiet confidence, both in the classroom and on the athletic field. At Lincoln, Mel also had a small, yet well-established circle of friends, who, like him, were consumed with sports and had been raised in families with little money.

Lincoln was a first-rate high school. It provided language classes in Spanish, French, German, and Hebrew. Lincoln's 5,000 students were predominantly Jewish and considered among the most talented students in the

New York metropolitan area. A large percentage of the faculty was Jewish, as was the case with many of the schools located in Jewish neighborhoods. Many students who attended Lincoln High in the 1930s and '40s would become well-known scientists, artists, and business executives. Two of its 1933 graduates culminated their distinguished careers with Nobel Prizes: Arthur Kornberg in physiology or medicine and Jerome Karle in chemistry. Joseph Heller, the author of *Catch-22,* was a 1941 graduate. The school also boasted excellent sports facilities. Above the state-of-the-art gym, a steeply banked running track was available for the team.

By this time, Mel had mastered juggling his interest in sports with his academic responsibilities and was, for the most part, a "B" student. But that is not to say he didn't experience a few bumps along the academic road. According to his friends, he was quiet and focused. He had a quick wit and a "great sense of humor, quick to laugh." Stanley Shapiro, a friend from his high-school days, describes Rosen as "always well liked, even then when we were high school kids. He never offended anyone. He was easy to get along with. As a person, Mel was always content. He was obviously raised well." Sol Saporta referred to Rosen as a "sweet guy, someone everybody liked, felt comfortable around. Even then you knew Mel was going to pursue some sort of career in athletics." Saporta adds, "Mel was my gambling buddy in those years."

Mel was also mature beyond his years. He'd already been working various jobs to help out at home. One was in a souvenir shop near the boardwalk in Coney Island, a colorful experience: "It was up to you as the salesman to size up your customer and see what price you could get. These hookers would come in with these Navy guys; it was easy to jump up the price because the guy was going to pay anything to please the gal. They would buy all sorts of prizes for their girlfriends. And then she would come back the next day and try and sell the prize back to us."

Mel's precocious development was likely an artifact of being given responsibility early in life since his mother was always working. She expected him to take care of himself, and when he entered high school he was expected to work to help with family expenses. While he had everything he needed— his mother made sure of that—he was still aware of their circumstances.

"We were poor but were never hungry. However, for my mother there was always anxiety, an uneasiness about what financial problems were right around the corner."

Even though today Rosen feels growing up without a father didn't create hardships for him, his friends feel otherwise. They remember him as popular but a little detached—his own man. "He always was well liked but usually he was on the periphery, the edges of our group," recalls Abe Becker, a close friend who became an accomplished basketball player at New York University in the 1940s. Neither Becker nor Stanley Shapiro ever visited Mel in his home and never met his mother or any other member of his family. Why? Mel and his friends spent most of their free time on the streets, hanging out, arguing sports, and gambling. The center of their universe was the streets of Brooklyn. "In New York City's working-class districts, Jews made the streets a second home."[29] In their neighborhoods the streets were a regular gathering place, providing New York Jews with a genuine sense of community with their neighbors. As well, Mel's living conditions didn't foster visits from friends. "We lived in a one-room apartment. Not exactly the best situation to bring friends home to. I focused on achievement. I enjoyed my friends. They were an important part of my life but I learned, growing up without a father, that to a certain extent I'd fend for myself. It set me apart a little bit."

Mel's independence and single-mindedness would contribute to his success as an athlete and a coach. He likely inherited these personality traits from his mother. Adele Peysner, Rosen's cousin, describes Mollie Rosen as a "take-charge person. A confident woman in control of her life, a person who made her voice heard in a group," as well as an "incredible cook and baker, whose *rugalach* were heavenly, made with a recipe she took to her grave." It was the warmth of the home created by Mollie and her unlimited love and pride that sustained Mel and fostered his rock-solid confidence throughout the different periods of his life.

Mel, slightly built and weighing a mere 110 pounds in his freshman year, elected not to try out for any of the varsity athletic teams at Lincoln. Competition for team spots was fierce. Mel competed instead on the intramural basketball and football teams. Mostly though, he concentrated on his schoolwork and finished the year with a solid "B" average.

In his sophomore year, Mel tried out for football, basketball, and baseball and learned quickly that making athletic teams wasn't going to be easy at a school with 5,000 students. "I went out for everything. First I went out for football. On the first play of practice some huge guy knocked me down. I thought, 'What the heck just happened?' On the next play I went out for a pass and he knocked me down again. I said to myself, 'Who needs this?' And that ended my football career. Then I went out for basketball. The first practice we ran wind sprints. I was very good. The second day we ran around the gym. I was terrific, even better. The third day we shot baskets and the coach took one look and cut me. Then I went out for baseball.

Lincoln High School's 1200-yard relay team finished second in the indoor city championships in 1944. From left: Jack Miniker, Mel Rosen, Gene Linderman, and Herb Fine.

On the first day of tryouts the coach told me to grab a bat and hit. The guy threw three straight fastballs right by me. I never took the bat off my shoulder. The coach yelled that I was never going to be a hitter, and he cut me at the end of the practice."

Herb Leber, a high school friend, remembers that Mel was a good track-man but not a very good all-around athlete. "He was not as coordinated as some and didn't have a great physique for sports. But he had extraordinary drive, an exceptional desire to excel, more desire than most."

AFTER MEL'S FRUSTRATING YEAR of tryouts, the way was paved for his track career at Lincoln High School. He made the track team his sophomore year. Hy "Doc" Schecter, one of the most successful coaches in Brooklyn, ran the track program. Schecter looked more like a college professor than a coach. He was a stocky, powerful man who wore wire-rimmed glasses and dressed in a sport coat and tie when teaching. His gray hair was cropped short. From the beginning, Mel was impressed with Schecter's meticulously scheduled workouts and the efficiency of his practices. Also impressive to Mel was how Schecter orchestrated the activities of large numbers of athletes. Schecter's workouts ran like clockwork. Rosen considers Schecter one of his coaching role models.

Schecter, a no-nonsense disciplinarian, realized immediately Mel was a better-than-average runner despite lacking the critical natural talent, the explosive speed, required of successful sprinters. But he saw that Mel possessed the necessary speed, endurance, and tenacity to compete successfully in middle-distance races, so he guided him to the 440-yard dash and the mile relay. He saw that Mel had superb technique: he was quick off the starting line and had a natural running style, the fundamentals that would provide a foundation for continued improvement. Most importantly, Schecter was impressed with Mel's enthusiasm for running, his unbridled motivation and coachability, and his highly competitive nature. Mel was one of those athletes who loved practice; he never missed showing up early for workouts. His success on the track was a basis for Mel to think about what lay ahead. "I loved the workouts. I enjoyed being around the coaches and other runners. It was then I began thinking about teaching school and coaching at the high school level as a career." When he wasn't working to perfect his own running technique, he would watch other runners and offer advice.

Mel, always realistic when evaluating athletic ability, understood early in high school that he would never become an elite runner. Thus he focused on how he could use his success in track to earn a scholarship to go away to school and become a physical education teacher and track coach. This was an important insight as he began to consider track as his ticket out of Brooklyn. He knew almost instinctively that if he stayed in Brooklyn he would end up like many of his schoolmates from high school hanging out on the corner day after day kibitzing, arguing about sports. Mel wanted more, and his way out might be a track scholarship. He began formulating his plan during his sophomore year at Lincoln High. He began considering different colleges, focusing only on those with successful track programs. "I knew getting a scholarship, particularly in track, would be difficult. There were few track scholarships to give, but I thought at a good track school, I would have a chance." During this time Mel became a student of the sport; he identified the best collegiate track teams and studied what it would take to get accepted and earn a scholarship. Planning to attend school away from Brooklyn created some anxiety, as he knew his mother expected him to remain home after graduating and find work as soon as possible.

Mel's sophomore and junior years at Lincoln were successful by any measure. He held a solid "B" average, was earning points at most track meets, worked various jobs, and helped out with the bills at home. He was voted co-captain of the track team in his junior year. That year, 1944, Lincoln placed first in the City Meet, beating Boys High School, a perennial powerhouse in track and field. Mel was a member of the 1200-yard relay, placing second. In the Brooklyn Invitational, he ran his best time ever in the 400. "It was my best race of the year. I ran a 52.8 and beat a guy from Boys High School. He was the best in the City. His name was Connie Ford and believe it or not years later he was on my staff that went to Japan and China to compete in the Eight Nation International Meet in 1980. I was head coach of the men's and women's teams. Our team was made up of Olympic athletes who never competed in the 1980 Olympics in Russia because of President Carter's decision to boycott."

Mel was also inducted into Athletika, an athletic and academic honor society, as its president. Athletika was tailor-made for a boy who, without a father, was looking for ways to prove himself. He began to understand the responsibilities for leadership. Schecter was counting on Mel leading Lincoln High to the City Championship.

LIKE MOST OF HIS friends, Mel didn't date but concentrated on school and sports, focusing his efforts to earn a scholarship. Gambling, however, continued to be important in his life. He and his friends frequented Chaim's Pool Hall, a Brighton Beach hangout that also served as a gambling house. Using his lunch money, he placed bets with the owner on all sorts of sporting events. Sol Saporta, former professor of linguistics at the University of Washington and Rosen's high school friend, recalls gambling with Mel: "All through high school we gambled there. Chaim was a bookie. We used to steal some of his gambling business and book sports events for customers who wanted to bet as little as 25 cents. This went on for some time until Chaim figured out we were stealing some of his business. As soon as he found out he kicked us out."

Abe Becker remembers: "Gambling in New York City was for some a way of life when we grew up. Mel and Sol [Saporta] were gambling quite a bit, as most of us were. It was a good thing our parents were unaware of what was going on. Even when I played summer ball in the Catskills, gambling was a big part of the entertainment for the workers and the hotel guests." However, despite its prominence, gambling was an illegal activity in New York, and it was considered a sin according to Jewish law and is forbidden. But for Jewish kids in Brooklyn in the 1930s and '40s it was one of the most popular activities.[30]

Growing up, Rosen knew the names of many of the infamous Jewish gangsters and gamblers of his era. Characters such as Abe Reles—a gambler who had turned state's evidence in 1940 and was thrown out of a sixth-floor window at the notorious Half Moon Hotel while under protective custody—and Arthur Rothstein, who controlled much of the illegal gambling on the Lower East Side and supplied the money (through his lieutenant, former feather-weight boxing champion Abe Attell) to fix the 1919 World

Series—were familiar names to Rosen and his friends. These names showed up in the newspapers frequently and served in some ways as role models. For Jewish boys in particular, gambling was an adventure, a way to rebel.

While Mel was always attracted to the emotional charge that was part of gambling, he gambled to win spending money and to help out at home. During those years, Mollie made ends meet only with financial help provided by her five brothers and four sisters; their support was a payback for all the sacrifices Mollie had made for them while they were growing up.

Mel grew up in a time when many Jewish children and their parents were experiencing "great conflict about how children should live, the language they should speak, and even their participation in sports."[31]

Sol Saporta put it this way: "Growing up in the 1930s and 1940s in Brooklyn, we knew our parents' way of life, a Jewish Orthodox way of life, wasn't for us. We rarely discussed Jewish issues except talking about Jewish sports figures of the time like Hank Greenberg and Nat Holman who was basketball coach at CCNY [City College of New York]. We identified with them. We were of the generation that wanted to make a life for ourselves, not patterned after the Orthodoxy of our parents. We had a Jewish identity without all the religious trappings."

Jewish children were beginning to identify with famous Jewish sports figures like those Saporta named and others like Marty Glickman, a Bronx native and member of the 1936 Olympic track team. However many Jewish parents who had recently come to America were unsupportive or uninterested in sports as they had come from a world where organized athletic events were unknown.[32] Thus, they deemed such activities as a waste of valuable time spent away from studying. Most Jewish immigrants of this era were small shop owners, tailors, watch repairmen, or farmers. While they often were not highly educated when they came to America, many spoke two or three languages. Mollie, for instance, while unable to read or write until she was older, spoke Russian, Yiddish, and English. Irving Howe described these immigrants' view of sports as "the pointlessness of play." Sports were deemed unimportant for Jewish boys and girls, unrelated to making a living, which for many parents meant studying to become a doctor, lawyer, or educator. Historian George Eisen noted, "Jews have always viewed sports participation as a means for achieving something else, gaining social status or scholarships to universities, or going into business—not an end in itself."[33] Red Auerbach, the former coach of the Boston Celtics, put it this way: "Jews just didn't aspire to careers in athletics. Sports were not the spheres in which Jews strove to excel."[34] As well, "American sports officials were oblivious to Judaism's clock and calendar."[35]

Rosen recounts a story about Irving Schmulowitz, a boy on his high school track team. Mel brought his friend's track uniform home Friday nights so Schmulowitz could go to synagogue Saturday morning, then after a short time sneak out, run to Mel's and change into his uniform and with Mel run to the track to compete in the track meet, a forbidden activity on the Sabbath for observant Jews. As Howe and Libo point out, while many Jewish immigrants wanted "to keep—for a time, at least—a balance between old and new, the cultural styles they brought with them and the cultural styles they encountered in the American cities," these conflicting attitudes created stress between immigrant parents and their children.[36]

Mel's mother, however, was interested in and supportive of her son's achievements both in the classroom and on the playing field. Because Mollie ran a secular household where there wasn't a traditional observance of the Sabbath and Jewish holidays, it was possible for Mel to participate in all aspects of a public school education, including sports. "She didn't say I couldn't play sports, but in no way could she relate to such activities either. She was just a Jewish mama who worried more about money than she worried about me playing games."

While Mel's education was Mollie's main concern, she was aware of his athletic pursuits and even attended one of his track meets in his high school junior year. It was the first time anyone in his family saw him compete. Unfortunately for Mel, her visit to his City Championship meet against their Brooklyn rival Erasmus High School wasn't what he would have hoped; he ran poorly and failed to place in the 440-yard dash. The entire spectacle for Mollie must have been confusing; the large crowds cheering young men running around a track for no apparent purpose. The event must have shaken her Old World sensibilities. Mel never talked about the track meet with her. But his interest in sports continued and became the central feature of his formative years, fueling his desire to earn a college scholarship as well as his coming to the decision in the ninth grade to become a physical education teacher and track coach.

Beginning in Mel's sophomore year, he worked summers in the Jewish resorts in upstate New York. Abe Becker recruited him to come to the Catskill Mountains and work as a busboy at one of the hundreds of Jewish resorts that dotted the countryside in upstate New York and New Jersey.[37] This geographical area, often referred to as the Borscht Belt, was the vacationland for Jews of all income levels eager to leave New York City during the summer months. It was also a place where high school and college students found well-paid summer employment. In the Catskill resorts, they could have a proper vacation like regular Americans, but they could do it in a very Jewish milieu.[38]

In his junior year, Mel traveled to Ellenville and applied to work as a busboy at Fallsview Hotel and Resort. The work was hard, but the money was good. The hotel staff was required to do their regular jobs and to provide entertainment to the guests as well. The young men were asked to play on the hotel's basketball team against teams from the other resorts in the area. These teams, representing the Jewish hotels and resorts in the Catskills, formed the famous Borsht Belt Basketball League, a training ground for players like Abe Becker, Sonny Hertzberg, and other well-known Jewish basketball players. "You were expected to play basketball and compete against teams from all over to provide hotel guests with games to watch. When I got there they saw I was a lousy player. The owner told me if I wanted a job I'd better be a good dancer. We danced with the teenaged girls and their mothers who were stuck there for the summer while the men stayed in the city and worked. The owners knew that if the girls were bored they'd go home. The owners tried everything to keep the paying guests there as long as possible." So Mel became a dancer to keep his job. Working seven days a week for the entire summer, and including his gambling winnings, he hoped to earn about a thousand dollars, enough to enter college in the fall. If he could earn a track scholarship, he might even be able to attend a college located outside of New York.

One weekend in his junior year, while he prepared for the Penn Relays, Mel's mother came to him with surprising news: "My mother told me she would be getting married over the weekend to Mr. Goldfarb. It was a shock to me because I'd never met him nor did I know my mother was seeing anyone. He was a sixtyish-year-old gentleman with three sons. He worked in the garment business and she told me when I came home from my track meet I should go to our new apartment at 1092 Willmohr Street in Flatbush." Mel was taken aback, as Mollie had never told him anything about Morris Goldfarb before that Friday night. However, Rosen looks on the bright side. "I was fortunate on two counts. First that my mother gave me the address before I left for the Penn Relays, and second, I remembered it!" Their new, one-bedroom apartment did not give the blended family of six much room. All four boys slept in the living room while Mollie and Morris occupied the bedroom.

Mel began his senior year with high expectations. Schecter made it clear to him and his teammates that he expected no less than a city championship. It was a time for Mel to increase his chances to earn a scholarship. At the end of the first term, however, he was declared academically ineligible; he had failed trigonometry and Hebrew. "I thought Hebrew would be an easy pass. After all, I knew the alphabet and some words and phrases." Mel's Hebrew teacher, a short beefy guy who was always dressed in a tie, rumpled white shirt, and dark jacket, taught his class with zeal. Rosen explains his problems with Hebrew this way, "My teacher had more interest in the Hebrew language than I did. I didn't take it seriously enough. Had I known then that I would one day go to Israel to coach in the Maccabiah Games, I would have studied harder." At the end of the first semester, when Mel learned of his failing grades, he immediately went to his trigonometry teacher, Mr. Baronoff, and asked if there was anything he could do to improve his grade so he could become eligible and graduate on time. Rosen remembers: "He was a man of few words; 'No,' he said, and that was that."

Coach Schecter was not pleased with his star runner, as he knew that without Mel's contributions in the 440-yard dash and the relays the city championship was probably out of reach. In fact, Lincoln finished second in the city championship meet that year. For Mel personally, ineligibility was a doubly terrible blow as it endangered his chances of a college track scholarship.

Mel was relegated to graduating a semester late, in January 1946. While Mollie attended his graduation ceremony, she didn't make a fuss over it. "My mom expected me to graduate. So she considered it no big deal. Also, because we didn't have the money, throwing a party was not high on her list. I think she felt my bar mitzvah party was enough."

Mel enrolled at Brooklyn College as a part-time evening student. There were two club track teams operating in the Brooklyn area at the time. The Pioneer Club recruited runners from all around the city and had mostly black athletes. The Grand Street Boys, a much smaller team, conveniently trained at Brooklyn College; Mel elected to run with them.

During the semester he spent at Brooklyn College, he wrote to the track coaches of five Big Ten schools, all with top mile relay teams: Iowa, Michigan, Indiana, Ohio State, and Illinois. This was a defining moment for Mel as he was taking steps to break away from Brooklyn and take control of his life.

In the summer of 1946, George Bresnahan, the head track coach at the University of Iowa, offered Mel a job in the school cafeteria to help cover his school expenses. Mel accepted the offer and immediately began planning his exodus from Brooklyn.

That summer, instead of working in the Catskills, he had a job as the children's table waiter at Goldman's Hotel and Resort in South Orange, New Jersey. His summer earnings and his job in the school cafeteria offered by Coach Bresnahan would provide just enough money to pay for his first year at Iowa. "After all," Rosen recalls, "I was used to getting by on little money. Growing up having very little was good training for how to get by." Tuition and room would cost $200 per semester.

Mollie, however, had a different idea of her son's future. She wanted him to graduate, get a job, and bring home a paycheck. At the very least, she hoped he would attend City College of New York, work part-time, and help out at home. Like the plans that many parents have for their children, hers didn't work out as she had hoped. Her son was going to Iowa.

"My mother and I were on good terms. There were no hard feelings. Like any Jewish mother, she was proud that I graduated from high school and was going to college, but she just wasn't excited about my leaving Brooklyn. She couldn't understand why I wouldn't go to CCNY since it was free. Of course she was a typical Jewish mama. You get your children finished with school, and they go out and work and put some money back into the house."

Despite the pressure exerted by Rosen's mother to stay in Brooklyn, he was confident his decision to attend Iowa was the correct one. "I knew my mother would be all right. She was a tough woman, a survivor. This was something I had to do even if it was difficult for my mother to accept."

While Mel would return to Brooklyn to visit during Christmas breaks and summers, he never had second thoughts about leaving. He was headed for the University of Iowa with enough money in his pocket for tuition and room. What mattered to him was that he was striking out on his own and breaking the influence of his family and community.

And what was going through his mother's mind? Disappointment, most certainly—her only child elected to break his ties and leave her behind in Brooklyn. In spite of her disappointment, however, she also must have reflected that it had only been 40 years since her parents had brought her to America with the promise of a better life. It was then Mollie most likely understood that the promise for her and her son had indeed been fulfilled.

2

No Looking Back

(1946–55)

"My mother never understood. She wanted me pushing carts in the Fashion District and helping with the bills."

On a hot and humid morning in August 1946, Mel Rosen boarded a train at Grand Central Terminal and headed west for Iowa City. Just as his grandparents had some 40 years earlier, he carried little, just a couple of bags and a few hundred dollars in his pocket, his savings from his high school and summer jobs. There were no going-away parties, no emotional farewells from family and friends, just his mother's disappointment that he would not be living and working in Brooklyn and contributing a paycheck.

Neither his mother nor her new husband, Morris Goldfarb, accompanied him to the train station. The journey towards assimilation that began with the Rosens and Kaminskys in the early 1900s continued as he stepped onto the train headed for America's Heartland. Travel on the New York Central and the Rock Island Rocket was only fitting: in Jewish literature, trains have been a metaphor for change, the coming of a new age.[1] The train ride was a break from tradition, and Rosen had a ticket in hand.

Rosen had once traveled with his mother and aunts and uncles to Washington, D.C., to see the cherry blossoms, but this was his first trip of more than a few hundred miles from home. The train was overcrowded so Rosen sat on a box in the aisle for the entire 15-hour trip. This minor discomfort didn't dampen his enthusiasm: he was headed for Iowa to begin a new chapter in his life. With each passing mile, Brooklyn and what it represented were left further behind. Attending the University of Iowa, Rosen felt, was central to realizing his dream to teach and coach at a high school and not end up pushing carts in the Garment District.

There was a festive mood on the train. The passengers were mainly military personnel returning home and college students traveling to campuses across the country. They were part of a great wave of veterans entering college on the G.I. Bill.[2] By 1946 more than 6,000 men and women were attending Iowa on the G.I. Bill. The university's president, Dr. Virgil Hancher, set the tone when he wrote, "Times of change are times of challenges. I trust that this university may help veterans of World War II to measure up to the challenge of the times."[3]

Rosen used his well-honed ability to fit in and passed the time on the long trip by talking with other passengers. "Most were my age. It was a pleasant trip. Looking out and seeing the landscape, I knew that there was no looking back. I was excited because I knew that if I worked hard anything was possible. That's how I was raised. I also knew Iowa was a long way from Brighton Beach and there might be a period of adjustment."

The mid-1940s marked a turning point for Jews of Rosen's generation as they "crossed a threshold to embrace the full promise by America. Before them stretched the American century," with all its possibilities.[4] Rosen wanted to explore beyond the Jewish neighborhoods of Brooklyn. His feelings were not unusual or unique. Many Jewish children were shaped more by the American culture they had learned about on the city streets than by the religious values of their parents. Unlike their parents and grandparents who were raised in the tightly segregated Jewish communities in central and Eastern Europe, those born in America spoke English, avoided European-style Orthodox synagogues, and were not drawn to the working-class world of Yiddish socialism.[5] Rosen and others of his generation did not deny their Jewish background, but rather this new, younger generation knew their Jewishness would be different than that of their immigrant parents.[6] They wanted to be Americans, not greenhorns.

Interestingly enough, in spite of the social forces pressing for change and assimilation, many Jews in New York during the postwar years were undergoing a religious revival. For example, "New York Jews founded more than

150 new congregations during these years. Why? They joined in order to associate with other Jews . . . and to demonstrate their commitment to ethnic survival."[7] The embracing by Jewish Americans of a new and stronger Jewish identity was a response in part to the growing awareness and understanding of the horrors of the Holocaust. Survivors who had migrated to the United States after the war didn't talk about their experiences in the camps, nor "was the world willing to listen" to the harrowing stories survivors had to tell.[8] Many survivors felt guilty they made it out alive while so many others perished. Many survivors didn't want to burden their children with stories about the camps. Thus, many American Jews were late in comprehending the horrific extent of the Holocaust.

Rosen never discussed the Holocaust with his mother or any of his friends in Brooklyn. "It wasn't until I got to Iowa that I became more fully aware of Nazi Germany and the Holocaust. We knew something happened to Jews in Germany and Poland, but we never imagined the scope of the genocide. I'm sure I lost family members from my mother and father's side. But I don't remember talking about this with my mother or any of my friends. It wasn't until I went to Israel for the first time in 1977 as coach in the Maccabiah Games and visited Yad Vashem, the Holocaust Museum in Jerusalem, that I began to understand the full extent of what happened."

Americans were on the move during the postwar years, and "American Jews began a journey that would rival the mass migration of their immigrant parents."[9] Much of that movement brought Jews from cities like New York, Chicago, and Los Angeles to smaller towns throughout America. The decision of some Jews to leave urban areas for small towns in other parts of the country charted a course towards assimilation. Rosen was part of this great migration.[10] "There was no doubt in my mind that I would fit in at the university. My mother and those of her generation may have had their doubts about being able to live away from the city, but I didn't. I never entertained that idea."

His train ride west was almost like a successful escape. "What I felt as I got on that train to Iowa was optimism. That if I applied myself everything would work out for the best. I didn't look back as the train pulled from the station. . . . I couldn't wait to get there and meet the coaches. After all, I had been thinking about this for a long time. I left Brighton Beach with a great sense of relief that I was able to get away."

Another factor fed this optimism. After the war Americans were feeling prosperous once again; there was an explosion of economic demand. "Four years of sacrifice had made Americans hungry for all the goods and services that had been denied them for so long."[11] The mood of uncertainty that had gripped the 1930s was now replaced with "hope and confidence in the future."[12] "In the aftermath of World War II, American Jewry seized upon America's promise to reinvent themselves."[13] Postwar America was indeed a land of opportunity. Rosen was riding the crest of this emerging change.

The future looked bright to Rosen; he'd taken his first steps toward realizing his dream, to run track at a major university and to become a high school teacher and coach. While Rosen was not of the mind to reinvent himself, he was determined to fit in and not allow his Jewishness to limit his opportunities.[14] "I never walked around with a star on my chest. America wasn't Poland during World War II. I never walked up to people and said, 'Hi, I'm Mel and I'm Jewish.' Nor did I ask people what church they belonged to. Those were topics I chose not to discuss."

ROSEN STEPPED OFF THE train in Iowa City around 11:00 at night. The town was closed tight except for a few taverns that bordered the campus, their neon signs casting an eerie light. The streets around the campus were deserted, as classes were not scheduled to begin for another two weeks. Rosen went to his assigned living quarters in the Quadrangle, a newly constructed housing unit. Exhausted from his long trip, he immediately fell into his bunk. Unlike the description of a Brooklyn G.I. who wrote of his first encounter with small-town Mid-America, "I was in a strange land among people who hardly spoke my own language,"[15] Rosen felt completely comfortable in his new place. He understood that Iowa City was not Brooklyn, but he remained singularly focused on his goal. "I knew lox and bagels would not be on the morning menu, but I just focused on getting started with school and running track as soon as I could. I knew this was my opportunity to make something of myself. No matter how hard the work it was going to be easier than pushing carts in the garment district. I felt lucky to have the opportunity."

While Iowa City was indeed not Brooklyn, it had its own Jewish history, a history similar to many small towns in middle America. In the mid-1800s German-American Jews left the urban centers to start family businesses in small towns. The diaspora that began with Eastern European Jews coming to America now continued through the 1940s and '50s as their children and grandchildren set out to find their piece of the American dream. These trailblazers often began their new lives as the only Jews in town. Most of these 19th-century small-town Jewish Americans were peddlers, small shop owners, and junk collectors.

While Iowa City was considered a progressive town, in part because of the influence of the university, both the university and the town had some difficulties adjusting to the presence of Jews and blacks. After World War II, Jews were beginning to be included in America's "triple melting pot"[16] of Catholics, Protestants, and Jews in small-town America. On the other hand, in the 1940s race relations between whites and blacks in Iowa were far from ideal. Segregation in Iowa was not formal; the state had one of the most progressive civil rights statutes in the United States. But the reality was that segregation existed: for example, housing for black families and black university students was relegated to certain parts of the town.

Rosen's Iowa teammate Keith Brown, a middle-distance runner and one of three African Americans on the track team, recalls the difficulty he had finding housing at the university. "My freshman year, I lived at home in Cedar Rapids and took the train each day to school. It was about a 30-mile trip and cost 30 or 40 cents. We were a poor family, and it was cheaper to take the train each day than it would have been to rent a room in Iowa City. In my sophomore year, I found a room to rent in the house of a local black family. I remember there were several of us students staying with them. In those days blacks, weren't allowed to stay in the university's dormitories. If you were black you had to find your own off-campus housing." The situation did not spoil Brown's experience at Iowa: "I was so happy to be going to school and running track that I really didn't think much about segregation. I just wanted to make something of myself."

Nonetheless, the separate housing policy for black students discouraged white and black students from socializing. "Once practice and classes were over the black athletes went to their rooms off-campus and the whites went to the dorms. It didn't foster relationships. Blacks mingled with blacks and whites mingled with whites," Brown recalls.

ROSEN WOKE EARLY THE morning after his arrival on the Iowa campus and went directly to the athletic offices and introduced himself to head track coach George Bresnahan. The coach was a tightly wound man of about 65 years of age and nearing the end of his distinguished career. Rosen noted Bresnahan's nervous mannerisms. "He was the kind of guy who couldn't keep still. If he wasn't moving from one place to another, his eyes were darting from one thing to the next. His hands were always in motion." Rosen would soon learn that the coach's nickname was "Jittery George."

Irrespective of the moniker, Bresnahan was an innovative coach and his athletes held him in high regard. Keith Brown remembers Bresnahan as "a man who knew his track. An excellent coach who worked well with all athletes, including the black athletes." Brown was rated the best half-miler in Iowa his senior year in high school. In spite of his outstanding ability, racism limited Brown's college opportunities. "In those times, in the 1940s, a lot of schools didn't recruit black distance runners. They were willing to recruit sprinters but not distance runners. We were pigeonholed. Coaches during that era were hesitant to recruit blacks for any event other than sprints. There were typically a limited number of scholarship spots for black athletes. If you were a middle distance man like me you didn't have as many opportunities for college. I was grateful for the opportunity Bresnahan was giving me."

Growing up poor without a father—like Rosen—Brown remembers the added burdens of racial discrimination in Cedar Rapids. "We didn't have it easy at home. My old man took off, just ran away. One day he just packed up and left us to fend for ourselves. We were a poor family trying to get by. Those were hard times. In a way I learned from my dad what happens when you don't live up to your responsibilities; others pay a price. I never forgot that lesson."

While there were no Jim Crow laws in Cedar Rapids and other towns in Iowa in the 1940s, "a color line did exist. Some eating places would not serve blacks and they found it 'convenient' to sit toward the back of buses to avoid hostility or confrontations."[17] Public schools in Iowa, while accepting black students, rarely hired black teachers for two basic reasons: racism and lack of African American teachers to choose from.[18]

Bresnahan was an aloof but innovative coach. Rosen said, "He never got real close with the athletes, but he was creative with his coaching techniques. He really promoted the track program and coached a number of Olympians over the years. He was on the 1928 Olympic coaching staff. Running for such a distinguished coach opens up your eyes to what is possible if you work hard. I was fortunate to have him as a coach, a role model. I learned quite a bit from Coach Bresnahan."

BRESNAHAN FOUND ROSEN TEMPORARY work helping Mrs. Olive Farr, the longtime head of the nursing program, to fix up her house. Rosen needed the work to cover expenses, as he wouldn't start his cafeteria job until the beginning of the semester, still two weeks away. Unfortunately his first job for Mrs. Farr did not end well. "She asked me to wash the walls in her house. She was the type of person who expected everything to be done to perfection. I started washing the wallpaper with lots of soap and water. The next thing I knew the coloring on the wallpaper began to run and the paper began to lift from the wall. Boy, did I ever run out of there. It was the fastest 400 I ever ran."

Once classes began and he got settled, Rosen's life quickly filled with work, study, and track practice. "I never had a chance to take advantage of Iowa City or the recreational activities the university offered. Every day I was up early to work at the cafeteria and have breakfast. Then I went to class and returned to the cafeteria to have lunch and work. After work I went to class again and track practice. Then as soon as practice was over, it was back to the cafeteria for my dinner and work. Nights I tried to study." Rosen's roommate was Bud Griesbach, the Illinois state high school swimming champion in the backstroke. Like Rosen, Griesbach worked in the school cafeteria to help pay for school. Iowa, like many schools of that era, had few scholarships to offer athletes in minor sports like track and swimming.

While Jews were accepted into general student life at Iowa, there remained obstacles preventing Jewish students from being fully integrated into the social fabric of the campus. The 25 Christian fraternities and sororities were off-limits to Jews, an exclusion not unique to Iowa; in the 1940s, the charters of many Greek-letter organizations explicitly barred Jews. The result was that "for the most part, the Greek system was closed to Jews, as well as blacks . . ."[19] This fact of life did not faze Rosen. "I wasn't a trouble maker and didn't make religion an issue." Rosen's strategy was to fit in and be accepted as a Jewish student athlete at Iowa.

Much of the social life for Iowa's Jewish students revolved around the Jewish fraternities Phi Epsilon Pi and Sigma Alpha Mu; a Jewish sorority, Sigma Delta Tau; and the Hillel, a Jewish student organization. Rosen had come to Iowa with some interest in pledging a Jewish fraternity. "When I was in high school I ran at the Penn Relays in Philadelphia and one night we went to a fraternity party and I thought that fraternity life looked interesting. But once I got to Iowa I quickly lost interest." Although he had friends in Phi Epsilon Pi, and often participated in the nightly poker game, he did not join. The reason was simple, "It cost a lot of money to join and I didn't have it. So that took care of that." But Rosen was ambivalent about joining anyway. "I had mixed feelings. I met some great guys and they had terrific poker games but I felt more comfortable mingling with a broad group of students. If I didn't have track maybe I would have been more interested, but I had my afternoons and weekends tied up with practices and meets. The track team was my fraternity, more or less. The bottom line was that I was at Iowa to run track and get a degree so I could make something of myself."

Rosen began his freshman year taking required courses in science, mathematics, and English. It was a difficult transition. While he got by with mostly Cs his first semester, Rosen struggled in the second semester and failed two courses. He was not put on academic probation and in spite of the rocky academic beginning, dropping out was not an option. "I never thought about leaving Iowa and going back home to work or go to school. When I went back to Brooklyn for the holidays and found many of the guys I had gone to high school with still standing on the same street corner, doing the same kibitzing, that made an impression on me."

Rosen made the cross-country team as a freshman. The season was relatively short, only five meets. Rosen placed in several of them and scored enough points to earn his freshman numeral. During the season, he got to know and understand Coach Bresnahan. It caught Rosen's eye that Bresnahan kept everyone who went out for the team. As long as the athlete came to practice faithfully and completed workouts, Bresnahan worked diligently with him—this was a practice Rosen later would follow as head coach at Auburn University (its name after 1960; previously it was Alabama Polytechnic Institute).

Rosen's most memorable race in cross-country his freshman year was a dual meet (a scored meet between two, three, or four teams) against Wisconsin, one of the strongest teams in the conference. "I made the travel team and it was my undoing. It was a four-mile race and when I hit the three-mile marker I saw the leaders were walking back toward me. They had already finished so I thought, why keep running? So I started walking back towards the finish line. One of Bresnahan's daughters, she was about 11 or 12, saw me and told her father I was walking. He was never the same with me again."

In spring Rosen joined the track team and focused on the quarter-mile and the two-mile relay. Although he didn't make the traveling squad to the Big Ten Conference meet, he did travel to Wisconsin, Minnesota, and Notre Dame and placed in several dual meets.

Rosen was declared academically ineligible for his sophomore year. He was not allowed to practice or travel with the team. "It was like being in exile. It was a difficult time for me. My sophomore year was not a good one, not being able to compete in track and cross-country. I remember two of the classes I failed my freshman year that caused me all the trouble, zoology and English composition. Zoology was too technical, and English composition required lots of writing which I didn't enjoy. You have to remember, I didn't have the academic support that athletes have now. It was just me against the world. Between practice and working three hours a day in the cafeteria, that didn't leave much time for studying."

In addition to a certain "Yiddishkeit," a love of Jewish culture, Rosen brought to Iowa the love of gambling he had acquired in Brooklyn where he and his friends would wager on sporting events. Rosen recalls, "Besides the money, gambling was a social activity. It was something Jewish kids, at least my crowd, just did." However, once he went away to college, that changed: "When I came to Iowa it was more to make quick money. Unfortunately when I lost I had to scramble to pay for school."

Rosen was well-suited to gambling, as he was very good with numbers. He could calculate odds quickly to determine his bets. Luck, however, could not be calculated. By the end of his freshman year, Rosen's gambling had escalated and become more of a problem for him. "I remember there was a football player, Duke Curran, who was running parlay cards on football games. I was a runner for him, collecting money from those placing bets on games. I'm sure he was making $200 or $300 a week. I got 25 percent of everything I collected. Then I took that money and used it for my own bets. If I ever hit I would have been in great shape. But I didn't."

The turning point came in his sophomore year. "I was gambling on all types of college and professional sports and making bets for others as well. Then I hit a really bad streak and lost all my money. I was left with nothing: no money for tuition, books. I had to call my sister and ask for a loan so I could continue in school. Asking for money was something I didn't want to do but I had little choice. When I spoke to my sister I felt so bad that right then and there I said to myself, 'Enough is enough.' I was betting big money, and it was driving me crazy. In the summers at the hotels I was betting $200 to $300 a night. I was working like heck, and I was throwing it all away. And that was the last time I ever placed bets. All of a sudden my life became easier, less complicated."

Rosen also understood that if he wanted to coach and teach he would have to stop gambling. Keith Brown saw a big change in Rosen. "When I first met Mel I knew he was into gambling and didn't spend a lot of time studying. But by his junior year he buckled down and became a good student. He was a smart guy and a good coach. He just needed to focus on his schoolwork to be successful."

WHILE ROSEN LEFT MUCH of his Jewish life back in Brooklyn, he was steadfast in his interest in meeting and dating Jewish girls. He knew that marrying outside his faith would have caused problems at home. "My mother couldn't have accepted that. Once I brought a Gentile girl home, and she got very upset. Such a thing would have created problems in my relationship with her." However, Rosen learned quickly the realities of the dating situation for Jews at Iowa. "I was a little shy about dating and didn't know how Gentile girls would feel about dating a Jewish guy. So I was hesitant to ask out a Gentile girl. After months contemplating my situation I finally got a date with a Jewish gal from the Jewish sorority. At the end of the night I told her I had a nice time and wanted to see her again, but she told me she was booked for the next four months! So I knew right then I wouldn't be dating many Jewish girls at Iowa."

Rosen attended the local synagogue in Iowa City several times, not so much for the religious service as to meet girls. "I went once or twice but there was no connection. After a couple of times I never went back." He then dated several Gentile women despite anxiety over how they and their parents might feel about a Jewish guy from New York, not to mention how his mother would have reacted. He invited several Gentile women to New York City on school breaks. To avoid confrontation with his mother, Rosen put up his guests at his sister's apartment just six blocks away.

The transition from living in Brooklyn, with its thriving Jewish infrastructure, to a predominantly Christian rural/small-town atmosphere with few Jews, could have posed problems. "People don't realize when you are raised in a place like Brooklyn, you don't go running all over New York City. You stay with your own little group." But Rosen, given his frequently changed living situations with his mother in Brighton Beach, was well-practiced in adapting to new arrangements. "At Iowa it was all country boys, right off the farm. It was a learning experience, but I got along fine. Those country boys accepted me. We didn't look for differences among ourselves as much as appreciating our differences."

ROSEN REGAINED HIS ELIGIBILITY his junior year. He was a much more motivated student, and his grades improved dramatically. His junior year was another turning point because Bresnahan retired and Francis X. Cretzmeyer was hired as the new head track coach. Cretzmeyer, an excellent runner in his day, had narrowly missed earning a spot on the U.S. team at the 1936 Olympics (known as the Nazi Olympics, when Jesse Owens triumphantly won four gold medals in front of Adolph Hitler). Where Bresnahan was fidgety and standoffish, Cretzmeyer was calm, warm, and approachable. While Rosen respected Bresnahan's coaching ability and got along with him, there never developed the close, personal relationship like he had with Hy Schecter, his high school coach. Rosen had missed that close mentoring. He and Cretzmeyer hit it off immediately.

Once eligible, Rosen wasted no time joining the cross-country team. He thought it would be good training for the track season and Coach Cretzmeyer was all for it. While the season went by uneventfully, Rosen made the traveling team and scored points in some meets, usually running just under 26 minutes for the four-mile course. He also developed a close relationship with Cretzmeyer that would prove beneficial in the upcoming years.

Rosen observed Coach Cretzmeyer manage racial issues that were part of everyday life in the 1950s. Traveling with an integrated track team often presented problems in pre-civil rights America. Ted Wheeler, an African American former distance runner at Iowa and eventually a coach there, has written about how Cretzmeyer protected his black athletes from the sting of segregation in the 1950s: "It was common practice that black athletes ate and roomed separately from other team members. In my sophomore year (1952) the Iowa track team took a sleeper train to the Kansas Relays. The train was the hotel while we competed in the relays, so the entire team stayed together. This seemingly simple act showed a respect for all members of Cretzmeyer's team and showed courage and grace on his part." Wheeler also remembers that Cretzmeyer refused to limit his black athletes to just the sprints despite the stereotypes of the day. "Consequently, in 1951 Iowa had the first black All American in cross-country and in 1952, the first black Olympic trial finalist in a distance race."[20]

Rosen recalls a different trip to Kansas. "We were going to the Kansas relays and Cretzmeyer stopped at some motel near a small town in Kansas. When Coach tried to check us in the owner refused to rent us rooms because we had several African American athletes on the team. When Coach

Cretzmeyer got back on the bus he didn't say a word, but we could see he was angry. We moved on. We all knew what happened, but he never talked to the team about it." Rosen has his own thoughts why Cretzmeyer didn't feel it was necessary to say anything to the team about the incident. "Athletes and coaches know that you are trying to win the meet—everything else is secondary. If you're coming down to run and you decide you won't run because of these reasons then we have wasted all our time and money. In athletics the way you get back and express your feelings is to win." After that Cretzmeyer was very careful to make reservations in advance with hotels that would accept his black athletes. By Rosen's senior year, Cretzmeyer was more successful recruiting black athletes from New York and Washington, D.C. "Some of the African American athletes came to Iowa because they felt being in the Big Ten Conference they wouldn't have to travel south for meets."

ROSEN'S SENIOR YEAR WAS his most successful athletically. Cretzmeyer switched him to the half-mile from the quarter-mile because he was getting injured frequently. The quarter-mile is an event that requires all-out speed, which puts the runner at greater risk for injury. It was a good decision; not only did Rosen stay healthy for the entire season, his running improved; his best time for the event was a respectable 1:59.8. He placed in several dual meets in both the 800-yard run and the one- and two-mile relays. Although Rosen didn't run in the Big Ten Conference Championship—the conference had only nine teams at the time as the University of Chicago dropped out in 1946 and Michigan State University didn't join until 1949—he placed in enough meets during the track season to win his letter jacket.

As his senior year wound down, Rosen began planning for graduation and seeking a high school coaching position.

Rosen graduated with a degree in physical education in June 1951. Mollie came to Iowa City to see him graduate, her first time visiting him at school. Her bothers and sisters helped pay for her train ticket. Rosen remembers the commencement and how his mother proudly sat through the entire ceremony. "The ceremony was unbelievably long. In fact, me and several of my friends left after about an hour. We couldn't take it. The speaker was Eric Johnson, Hollywood's movie censor. He was interesting for the first hour or so but after that we just left. When I saw my mother after the ceremony she looked tired and confused. I don't think she understood what was happening, but I could tell she was very proud. Her son was a college graduate."

Rosen ultimately decided to enter graduate school and work towards a master's degree in physical education. "At the time, they were drafting people. If you had a student deferment you could stay out. Given those circumstances, the classroom looked awfully good!" Rosen entered the Iowa masters' program in physical education in the fall of 1951. Graduate school allowed him to complete an internship as a track coach at University High School in Iowa City. "I still figured I would end up a high school coach so the internship was necessary to complete my teaching certification." Rosen had a successful year coaching at University High. The team finished second in the state track meet, quite an achievement for a first-time head coach who

Graduate assistant Mel Rosen (first row, far left) with members of the University of Iowa cross country team, 1952. Coach F. X. Cretzmeyer stands behind him.

had just graduated from college. It gave Rosen his first taste of winning as a coach, and he liked it.

That year Rosen also got his big college coaching break, when Cretzmeyer offered him a graduate assistantship for $100 a month (dramatically improving his financial position) to help coach the track and cross-country teams. Thus began a two-year coaching tutelage under Cretzmeyer. Rosen was assigned to work with the sprinters and middle-distance runners. Cretzmeyer and Rosen formed an excellent team. Under their leadership, Iowa won the 1600 relay and placed fifth overall in the indoor Big Ten Conference meet. Rosen played a big role in coaching Ted Wheeler, the previously mentioned miler who would later make the 1956 Olympic Team, and Deacon Jones (not the future NFL football star of the same name), who would run the steeplechase at the same Olympics.

It was at this time that Cretzmeyer and Rosen first instituted interval training, a training approach in which each workout session consists of intense exertion alternating with periods of lighter exertion or rest. Interval training is designed to build strength and endurance. Rosen had been following the success that interval training was having on the performance of Emil Zatopec, a Czech long-distance runner best known for winning three gold medals at the 1952 Helsinki Olympics.

Rosen completed his master's degree at Iowa in June 1952. Riding the wave of his academic success, Rosen began taking coursework for his doctorate in physical education. Because of Iowa's stellar reputation in physical education, the graduate program attracted students from all over the country. Eddie Robinson, who became a legendary football coach at Grambling, attended graduate school at Iowa in the early 1950s, and earned his master's degree in 1954. He coached Grambling for 56 years and became one of the most successful coaches in NCAA history. Robinson caught Rosen's eye. "You could tell this guy was unique. He had the intelligence and the drive to be a great coach."

Rosen said he had been unaware of it when he enrolled in 1946, but "Iowa had one of the best physical education departments in the country. They were well known for doing research. In fact, one reason I was able to get a job at Auburn was on the strength of the physical education department."

At Fort Dix with his mother and Goldfarb, 1953.

Rosen was drafted by the United States Army in June 1953, "not the best day of my life." He went home to visit his mother for a couple of weeks before he had to report to Fort Dix, New Jersey. He then completed the full range of aptitude testing required of all recruits and qualified for Officers Candidate School (OCS) located at Fort Benning, Georgia. His commanding officer, however, asked Rosen to stay at Fort Dix and join the counterintelligence unit. Rosen declined the offer because OCS paid more and he could thus send more money home to his mother. Rosen was transferred to Fort Benning, and it was not a good fit. "I knew two minutes after I arrived that OCS was not for me. I heard all the yelling and screaming and knew I had to get out. I went to the commanding officer and asked if I could be reassigned to another unit. Well, all I heard from him for the next 20 minutes was screaming and profanities. It took about four weeks for them to finally reassign me." One other incident left a bad taste for Rosen. During one of their routine marching and formation exercises, a sergeant, not liking Rosen's marching technique, ran up to him and screamed, "You people never follow directions. You people always go your own way." "I knew what he meant. The guy was anti-Semitic. He didn't like Jews."

Rosen was designated as a recreational specialist based on his athletic and coaching background, and was assigned to coach the regimental track team. He had quick success; his team won the post meet. Based on that success, Rosen was promoted to head coach of the post team. Some of Rosen's Army athletes had been accomplished collegiate track stars. Pete Retzlaff, who threw the discus and shot, starred at the University of South Dakota and later played for the Philadelphia Eagles. Stan Chelchowski returned to MacNeese State University after his military service and became an elite distance runner. Rosen worked extensively with pole vaulter Lyle Dickey, who attended Oregon State University and would win the 1956 NCAA Championships. (In a roundabout way Dickey played a role in Rosen later getting the Auburn coaching job. Rosen traveled with Dickey to Auburn several times to use their pole-vaulting and training facilities. During these visits Rosen met Wilbur Hutsell, who was then in the final stage of his long and distinguished career as head track coach at Auburn.)

Life at Fort Benning was an adjustment for Rosen. This was his first experience living in the South. Fort Benning during the 1950s was going through significant changes. The onset of the Korean War had been the impetus for the armed forces to integrate all training and combat units, including those in the South. By the time Rosen served in 1953, 95 percent of African American soldiers were serving in integrated units.

But old habits and thinking patterns die hard, and racial prejudices and tensions were part of everyday life at Fort Benning. Don Johnson, who ran for Rosen at Fort Benning for a short period before being sent overseas, and who would run for Rosen at Auburn in 1957, remembers integration at Fort Benning. "I grew up in Bessemer, Alabama. One day at Fort Benning we were told by our commanding officer we would be merging with an all-black unit. He told us we had better not cause problems when the units were integrated. It was a new experience living in the barracks together and working alongside blacks. It took time to get used to."

In spring 1954, Rosen was invited by the track coach at Tuskegee Institute (now Tuskegee University) to bring his team over for a dual meet. Tuskegee had excellent track teams and was a natural opponent given its proximity to Fort Benning. Tuskegee, a historically black university located in east Alabama, was about an hour's drive from the army post. Rosen remembers, "A week or so before we were scheduled to go, a group of five white athletes, all from the South, came to me and said they were 'uncomfortable' competing against black athletes and were not going to take the trip. They weren't nasty about it but matter-of-fact. At first it caught me off guard. I knew it was pointless to try to change their minds. Their attitudes were embedded. So I just left them behind. I had several black athletes, and they knew what was going on, but they never said anything about it and I didn't either. I focused on getting prepared to win the meet. I think the black athletes on the team were very familiar with such things and learned to deal with it. We never discussed it. The whole thing just reflected the times and the location." As it turned out, the trip was a success; Rosen's team won the meet and there were no problems during the Tuskegee trip. The incident did not alter Rosen's scheduling practices, however. He stood firm and continued to schedule meets with integrated teams. Rosen felt his trip to Tuskegee was significant as it gave him a clear picture of coaching in the Deep South. "I think we were the only sports team at Fort Benning to ever compete at Tuskegee. It wasn't easy to get permission for the trip. The black athletes on my team had considerable pride going to Tuskegee. The trip gave me insight into the racial politics of the South. Tuskegee Coach Cleve Abbott was a gracious host. The best part of the meet for me was we won!"

Rosen's time at Fort Benning prepared him for some of the challenges he would face coaching at Auburn—how to bridge the racial divide. "Being stationed at Fort Benning you saw instances of racism that made you think and clarify your own values. I think being Jewish made me especially sensitive about that." Don Johnson, who was among the group of five who refused to travel to Tuskegee says, "You have to remember the time and place. Many of us from the South had not experienced integration. It was an uncomfortable experience for us."

There were significant racial problems off-base as well. One day Rosen and a group from the post took a bus into Columbus, Georgia, to see a movie. When they boarded the bus for the 20-minute ride back to Fort

Benning, the driver refused to drive. After a few uncomfortable moments, he finally told them that until that "nigger" moved to the back, he wasn't going to start the bus. "We just sat there as the guy got up and moved to the back and said nothing; no one said anything. I remember it was a very quiet ride back to the base."

Private First Class Rosen was discharged from the Army in March 1955 and returned to Iowa to continue work on his doctorate. He had finished most of the required coursework and lacked only the dissertation to complete the degree. But Dr. C. H. McCloy, head of the physical education department, strongly advised Rosen to leave the program and work to gain teaching and coaching experience before he finished his degree. McCloy's advice and Rosen's own waning interest in school prompted him to look for a job. "It was the best advice possible. I didn't have an interest in continuing the doctoral program and it was time to get to work. I was getting to be a professional student."

In August 1955, Rosen learned of a job teaching gymnastics at Auburn University. While Rosen had little experience teaching gymnastics, he figured he could learn the sport quickly. He immediately called the head of the search committee, Arnold "Swede" Umbach, chair of the physical education department. Rosen drove to Auburn to interview for the position. "In those days there weren't big search committees. In my case, Coach Umbach made the decision to hire me. We spent the day together and he basically showed me all of the athletic venues." At the end of the day, Umbach offered Rosen the job. "When I asked Coach Umbach what the salary was, he said $3,360. I asked, was that per month, and he told me no, per year! I took the job immediately as I thought it might help me get into the coaching business." It was a match of convenience in some respects; Rosen was nervous he would not be able to find a job at such a late date before the fall term began, and Umbach was a little desperate himself: his two gymnastics instructors had resigned unexpectedly, and he needed a replacement quickly.

Rosen was lucky to find a position at a Southern university. In the 1950s many universities were still largely anti-Semitic, and some schools, particularly in the South, wouldn't hire Jewish faculty.[21] But Rosen's religion was not mentioned by Umbach or any of the other coaches he met during his interview. "When I came for the interview I thought that being Jewish might have a negative impact on my chances of getting the job. But I was wrong. Coach Umbach was the kind of guy who didn't care about your religion but just your ability to do the job you were hired to do."

Rosen went home to Brooklyn to visit his mother before heading south. Mollie was thrilled he had an appointment. "I don't think she knew where Auburn, Alabama, was. All she knew, her son was finally earning a paycheck. That it was in gymnastics—she knew from nothing about gymnastics."

His Brooklyn friends were shocked that he was going to live in Auburn. Abe Becker recalls telling Rosen, "Be careful down there. The South isn't the best place to be for a Jew." Rosen didn't care; he was finally employed. He didn't come to Auburn with a chip on his shoulder. "I was thankful to have a job. Besides, my philosophy is don't go looking for trouble; you just might find it." Rosen was not concerned about the lack of Jewish life in Auburn. "This was never an issue with me. I mean, I was with all Gentiles in the army, I ran with all Gentiles at Iowa. I was used to it. I knew how to get by. I tried to get along with everyone and concentrate on teaching my classes." He took a practical approach to his situation: he needed a job, and Auburn gave him his start. Rosen was counting on parlaying teaching gymnastics into a coaching position with the track team. And the main player in his plan was head track coach Wilbur Hutsell.

IN AUGUST 1955, ROSEN gathered a few changes of clothes and personal items, packed it all into the 1946 Chevy he had just purchased for $200, and headed south to Auburn, Alabama. He had a few hundred dollars in his pocket, about the same amount he had when he left Brooklyn for Iowa nine years earlier. Rosen knew teaching gymnastics was not the job he wanted. He was sure he could somehow obtain a track appointment once on the faculty. He wanted to coach, and Auburn, a Southeastern Conference school, was as good a place as any to begin.

As he drove south through the Carolinas, Georgia, and into Alabama, Rosen couldn't help smiling to himself as he thought how Mollie, the consummate Jewish liberal and one-time member of the International Garment

Workers Union, would react to the evangelical Christian Deep South when she came for her first visit.

Mel Rosen was 27 years old, single, and had no qualms about heading south and starting his teaching career. In fact, never had he felt more excited about the challenges ahead.

A Plan of His Own

(1955–63)

"All I thought about was that the heat was good for running. A great place to train collegiate athletes."

When Rosen came to Auburn in August 1955, it was the quintessential small, Southern town. Located in the Bible Belt, Auburn had a population of just 15,000 residents, 15 percent of whom were black. Auburn University (then named Alabama Polytechnic Institute), was a land-grant university established in 1854 and a century later enrolled 9,000 students. Religion played an important role in most peoples' lives. Predominantly Southern Baptists and Methodists, their church affiliations served as the foundation for friendships and business relationships. Often the first question asked a newcomer was, "Where do you go to church?"

Ironically, Sunday in Auburn, as in most places, actually, was the most segregated day of the week. Housing in Auburn was segregated as well. Many black residents lived in the northwest part of town across the railroad tracks. The public schools were also segregated. Despite the 1954 *Brown v. Board of Education* U.S. Supreme Court ruling that states could not lawfully segregate school children by race,[1] Auburn public schools would remain essentially segregated for another 15 years, until 1969. As one black resident of the time stated, "Auburn was a friendly town, as long as you weren't black."

While Auburn appeared a tame, quiet town on the surface, there were undercurrents of white anger regarding the inevitable coming of desegregation. In Auburn and throughout the South, White Citizens' Councils— essentially white-collar KKK groups—sprang up after *Brown* to combat integration. Henry Stern, a local Jewish business man, remembers attending such a meeting in Opelika. "Several in the business community invited me to attend. I only went once or twice because I didn't like what was said at the meetings. I didn't want to be associated with racism, even though there was pressure to attend." It was telling about Jewish assimilation in Auburn that Stern was not only invited to these meetings, but expected to participate.

The *Brown* ruling was widely detested in the South. A 1956 public poll tracking reaction to the Supreme Court decision found that 90 percent of Southern whites disapproved. This attitude sometimes translated into violence. From the day the Supreme Court ruled in *Brown* "until the end of the 1950s, hundreds of homes, schools, and houses of worship across the South exploded."[2]

THIS WAS THE ATMOSPHERE that greeted Rosen as he began his teaching career at Auburn University. "The South was going through changes. Even though Auburn was a small town and off the beaten path, it too was changing. Sometimes when you are in the middle of things you don't have the perspective to understand its significance. My biggest worry was to figure out how to teach gymnastics, a sport I knew little about."

Rosen was assigned seven classes. It was a heavy teaching load, but he didn't complain. Although he was happy to be employed as a gymnastics instructor, he wanted to coach track. Soon after he began his teaching duties, he called head track coach Wilbur Hutsell, the dean of Southern track and field coaches, asking if he could serve as his assistant. Hutsell said there was no money in the athletic budget to pay for an assistant but he'd let Rosen know if the situation changed. Hutsell was speaking the truth; money was tight. Ticket sales for the entire 1955 season amounted to a mere $24; the track program lost almost $7,000. Rosen understood the financial problems. "You have to remember Auburn was a poor school in the 1950s. There was very little money going into the track program. Coach Hutsell scrutinized every dollar spent."

What Rosen didn't know at the time was that despite the limited funds, Hutsell did want an assistant and was capitalizing on his long-standing relationship with Jeff Beard, the athletic director, and Shug Jordan, the head football coach, to secure the necessary funding. For 34 years Hutsell had run the track program as a one-man operation. He was approaching 65 and the years were catching up to him. Along with his responsibilities as head track coach, he sometimes served as trainer for the football team and worked closely with Coach Jordan. He had also served three stints as athletic director, a stressful and time-consuming responsibility he didn't enjoy. In a 1949 letter, he complained, "I was demoted and made athletic director." He went on, "An A.D.'s job does not carry the enjoyment that goes with the training of a bunch of boys."[3] Nevertheless, as athletic director, Hutsell took his assignment seriously and followed rules scrupulously. Artie Shaw, a well-known band leader of the era, was contracted to perform at halftime of the 1949 Auburn-Alabama football game. One of Shaw's representatives asked for a sideline pass so Shaw, an avid football fan, could watch the game from the field. Hutsell, citing a long-standing rule, wrote: "Both Auburn and Alabama are in agreement that only players, staff members, and members of the freshman football squads shall be on the sidelines at the time of the game. It would be impossible for us to add even one person to this sideline list without letting down the bars entirely."[4]

Most coaches in the Southeastern Conference in the 1950s, particularly those guiding spring sports, were assigned multiple coaching responsibilities. Hutsell was putting in long workdays, and he was no longer a young man. He wanted a full-time assistant to lighten his workload. Fred Carley, Hutsell's graduate assistant in 1954–55, who had run for Hutsell and placed sixth in the mile in the 1946 NCAA track championships, was graduating. Hutsell was not happy with the prospect of coaching without the aid of an assistant, nor was the idea of training another graduate student appealing. Hutsell wanted a more stable, long-term arrangement than a graduate assistant who would graduate in a year or two and leave for employment elsewhere. He felt he'd earned the right to have a full-time assistant after all the years he contributed to Auburn's athletic department.

The heat was oppressive as Rosen settled in that summer of 1955, but it mattered little to him. "All I thought about was that the heat was good for running. A great place to train collegiate athletes."

Rosen's first residence in Auburn was a boarding house located just blocks from campus. His rented room cost $25 a month. He took his meals a few blocks away at Mrs. Walters' Boarding House—"the best eating in town," Swede Umbach had told him—for an additional $25 a month. "I ate with about 10 good old Southern boys. I remember I was the main guy because I was at the head of the table and passed all the food. I had never seen food like that. I hadn't eaten grits yet. So I just kept passing the food until I saw something I could nibble on, which didn't happen with much frequency. I didn't starve, but it was an experience. I would have given anything then for a Nathan's hot dog or a corned beef sandwich."

By early 1956, Rosen was resigned to the likelihood that he wouldn't get an appointment as assistant track coach at Auburn. "I gave up on the track situation because Hutsell said he couldn't do anything. If he couldn't pull strings, then it wasn't going to happen. I started looking around. I wrote to the University of Michigan at Flint and went up there for an interview as they had an opening in track and gymnastics. I also wrote to Berea College in Kentucky."

But in March, with no warning, Hutsell asked Rosen if he was still interested in being the assistant track coach. He offered Rosen a $60 a month raise. Rosen accepted immediately; he knew Hutsell wasn't going to negotiate the salary, even if he used another coaching offer as leverage. "If I brought up the prospect of another job to increase my salary, I think he would have shook hands with me and wished me luck, and he would have said, 'bon voyage.' That was Coach Hutsell. He was a man of few words."

Rosen was elated with the opportunity, but he kept one concern to himself: Auburn's segregated campus and sports programs. Auburn won the SEC conference meet in 1954 and 1955. But despite these successes, the SEC was changing, and Auburn needed to change with it to continue to be successful. He knew Auburn couldn't compete at the national level without black athletes.

Rosen understood that Hutsell wasn't going to make any groundbreaking decisions about recruiting black athletes. He felt it wasn't Hutsell's nature to take such professional and personal risks. Hutsell had been at Auburn for 35 years and it was unlikely he would now change the way he did things. Hut-

Coach Wilbur Hutsell after 42 years as head track and field coach at Auburn (courtesy of Auburn University Special Collections and Archives).

sell wanted to insure his legacy, not get embroiled in a controversy regarding recruiting black athletes. Rosen thought Hutsell was too cautious to move Auburn's program ahead, and felt that if he were ever lucky enough to be appointed head coach, he would need a plan to move the program forward in a deliberate, progressive direction.

HUTSELL AND ROSEN WERE a successful coaching team from the beginning. Both were outstanding men. Born in 1892 in Moberly, Missouri, Hutsell lettered in track at the University of Missouri and graduated in 1919. After completing several coaching assignments, he became coach of the Birmingham Athletic Club. After two years in Birmingham, he was named the first head track coach at Alabama Polytechnic Institute in 1921. Track already had an informal but established niche at Auburn. From 1895 until Hutsell arrived on campus, the university's team was composed of a small group of male students who coached themselves. Each year they elected a team captain who served as unofficial coach. In 1921 Hutsell formalized the men's track and field program. With the help of some friends, he built the first track at Auburn, a fifth-mile dirt oval,[5] that was used until a new track was built in Cliff Hare Stadium in 1940—it is fair to say that Hutsell literally built Auburn's track team from the ground up.

While Hutsell was formal, a bit standoffish, and all-business, Rosen was voluble, with a biting sense of humor that complemented Hutsell's dry wit. Hutsell's manner was small-town rural South, while Rosen retained his New York edge. Their relationship was highly proscribed; they spoke of nothing but track. Neither man initiated discussions about politics or religion. "These topics were off limits. If we had ever discussed politics or religion there would have been disagreements that would have had a negative impact on our relationship. Coach Hutsell was a great guy, a great coach, but he did not want to be challenged about his political or personal views."

On the field, Hutsell was concerned that his team was weak in the sprints and needed improvements.[6] He knew exactly how he wanted to use Rosen's talents. He put him in charge of the sprints, relays, and distance events. Rosen's mentor, Francis Cretzmeyer, had prepared him for this new coaching assignment. Rosen had learned from Cretzmeyer not to overwork his athletes; underworking sprinters, especially, meant that runners were rarely sidelined with injuries. Rosen also increased their work on form running to improve technique, and less on speed drills.

Finally, Rosen increased practice time for interval training, again emphasizing not overworking and risking injury. Interval training was in vogue in Europe, and he and Cretzmeyer had used it at Iowa. The changes that Hutsell and Rosen instituted were considered innovative, and the results were immediate. In the 1956 SEC championships, Auburn placed second behind Florida. In their best showing in years, Auburn's 400-meter relay captured second place, just behind LSU. Auburn got superior performances from Dave Powell in the 880, Don Johnson in the 220 and 440, Bill Yarbrough in the broad jump, and Ellsworth Richter in the mile and two-mile.

Hutsell allowed Rosen to work independently. For the eight years Rosen served as assistant coach, Hutsell didn't second-guess Rosen's decisions. Whether it concerned training schedules Rosen developed, or how he selected runners for the relays, Hutsell never interceded. "I knew Coach Hutsell wanted what any coach wanted—to win. We avoided injuring our athletes during practice by not overworking them. That was a rule I followed throughout my career, even when I was the Olympic coach. An injured runner is not going to score points. Hutsell liked to analyze practices once the athletes left for home. Most evenings we talked for a couple of hours after practice."

Hawthorne Wesley, a middle-distance runner from 1955 to 1957 who placed second in the 1956 SEC conference meet in the two-mile, saw Rosen begin his assistant coaching duties. There was a transition period, both for Rosen and the athletes. "It took a little time to get used to Mel, with his New York accent and his dry, biting sense of humor," Wesley remembered some 55 years later. "We were not used to his style. Some of the athletes on the team were unhappy with the switch to Mel. It took some time for Mel to adjust as well, to tailor his coaching style to the Southern athlete as many of them came from small towns. From the start Mel was mature and thoughtful, and, over time, gained the confidence of the athletes."

Rosen was 28 when he was appointed assistant coach, not much older than some of the athletes. But he was mature beyond his years. At least part of his maturity can be attributed to Mollie. She had always expected him to take care of himself growing up in Brighton Beach. In return, throughout his adult years, Rosen sent money home to help support Mollie. Rosen was comfortable with responsibility and never shied away from it.

While it did take Rosen time to win the confidence of the athletes, by the middle of his first year he was putting his own stamp on the team. They began to trust his judgment, especially where training and technique were concerned. Dave Powell, captain of the 1955 squad and a Hutsell protégé, wrote Rosen years later expressing his gratitude: "Because Coach Hutsell was my head coach, I am not sure I ever mentioned it to you, and if not, I should have, you were a tremendous inspiration to me during my senior year. I think you were responsible for getting out of me every ounce of speed that my frail body was capable of. I particularly remember seeing you at the 660 mark with your watch calling out the time. To this day I often think of you at the beginning of the turn urging me to run faster."[7] As this letter shows, Rosen was relentless in urging his athletes on and influencing them. Importantly, Hutsell was secure enough to let Rosen develop runners as he saw fit.

Rosen had easily adjusted to his new teaching and coaching assignments. He performed many duties as assistant coach, some more glamorous than others. Not only was he responsible for developing workouts but he also served as recruiter, albeit one with no budget for scholarships to woo prime athletes. He had an unusual recruiting strategy for these difficult circumstances: "Every year I went to the Alabama high school championships and rooted against the athletes I wanted to bring to Auburn. A second or third place suited me just fine. I knew if they didn't win their events, Alabama and the other schools with scholarships to give would be less inclined to recruit them. I think I was the only coach in the country who rooted against the athletes I wanted to bring to Auburn. That's how you recruit without a budget."

While Rosen was given responsibility for team discipline, there were few problems that required his intervention. "You have to remember, when you have mostly walk-ons, you don't have as many discipline problems. Non-scholarship athletes are on the team because they want to be. Track is such a demanding sport that an athlete has to be motivated to participate for no scholarship money. We had people like Ellsworth Richter, Hawthorne Wesley, and Dave Powell who made the most of their ability because they worked so hard. With athletes like that, discipline is not usually a problem."

Occasionally Rosen had to exercise his authority. In 1958, on a team bus trip to the Florida Relays, Rosen, the one-time gambler, had to deal with the aftermath of a card game. Several of the athletes had been playing poker in the back of the bus, a practice that Hutsell and Rosen allowed. Long jumper Tom Hollingsworth lost all his money. By the time the team arrived in Gainesville, all he could think about was getting back on the bus and winning back his money. "Hollingsworth lost everything, including his meal money. I remember how upset he was about it. When the meet started I could see Hollingsworth was not going to be much help to us. He was too distracted. He lost the long jump, an event he should have won. It was then I made a rule that there could be no gambling on the team bus. I figured I saved Hollingsworth several hundred dollars, as he must have been a lousy poker player."

Sometimes, however, circumstances required Rosen to temper discipline.

Jim Dozier, who ran for Hutsell from 1960 to 1962, saw Hutsell and Rosen develop their professional relationship. Because Rosen was closer in age to the athletes than he was to Hutsell, Dozier observed Rosen trying to keep the peace between the "old school" head coach and the team. On a bus trip in 1961, several team members taped a *Playboy* centerfold to the ceiling of the bus. If the gentlemanly Hutsell had seen the picture, he would have been beside himself with anger. The athletes were not much worried because Hutsell's eyesight was poor and an old neck injury would not allow him to tilt his head upward to see the centerfold. Rosen, however, did see it, and, as Dozier remembers, just shook his head and concentrated on keeping Hutsell's attention diverted.

Occasionally Rosen faced even more unusual situations. "We had a sprinter in 1957 named Jimmy 'Red' Phillips. Phillips was an All American football end whom Coach [Shug] Jordan gave permission to run track. Phillips was versatile, weighed 200 pounds, and competed in the shot, javelin, and the 100-yard dash. At one meet he was getting ready to run the 400-meter relay and he came up to me right before the race and took out his teeth and asked me to hold them until the end of the race. I screamed, 'Are you crazy?' I told him to put them under the goalpost and they would be there until after the race. Being an assistant coach is not glamorous. But the important thing is our relay team won the race. In spite of Red's victory, I let him retrieve his own teeth."

Phillips was a finicky eater. He didn't like roast beef, a staple on Hutsell and Rosen's pre-meet meal. "Red complained he wanted steak. I told him if he wanted steak to win the conference championship and we could discuss his meal plan."

THE EIGHT YEARS ROSEN served as Hutsell's assistant were successful by any standard. The team accomplishments included 19 first place medals in the SEC Championships; a 1961 SEC conference team championship; two second-place conference performances and four third-place finishes. These statistics were especially impressive for a coaching staff competing with a team of primarily walk-ons. Dave Powell won the 1956 conference in the 880. Powell was a natural leader whose training habits made others on the team better. One who was influenced by Powell was Ellsworth Richter, a walk-on who won the two-mile in the 1956 and 1957 conference championships. Richter didn't look like a great athlete. "He ran on his toes, straight up and down. He didn't look good. When his opponents saw Richter warm up I'm sure they figured he'd be an easy victim. But they found out he could run!" Richter was Rosen's first athlete to win an SEC championship.

Another outstanding performer on the 1957 team was Bill Yarbrough, a walk-on from Atlanta. Yarbrough was a stocky, powerful runner at five feet nine inches tall, short for a hurdler, but he made up for it with speed. He won the SEC championship high hurdles and placed second in the long jump and high jump.

Hindman Wall won the SEC javelin competition in 1958, the only individual conference championship Auburn won that year. Wall, one of Auburn's most versatile athletes, also played football and baseball. In fact, Rosen first spotted Wall on the baseball diamond. "I saw he had a great arm. He wasn't an accurate thrower, but he could throw the thing a mile. We knew if Hindman could throw a baseball 300 feet, then he could throw a javelin around 200 feet. Why was 200 feet important? Because a javelin throw of about 200 feet could win the SEC championship." Wall did just that. He was the 1958 conference champion in the javelin with a throw of 210 feet. Wall eventually became athletic director at Auburn.

Richard Crane, one of Auburn's all-time dominant discus throwers, won three conference championships, 1959–61. He also won the shot put in 1959. Crane was an athlete ahead of his time. At six feet four inches tall and 210 pounds, he towered over most of his track competitors. He also studied his sport. He had read that weightlifting would help a track athlete increase performance, so he spent much of his time in the weight room working out with football players. However, while Hutsell promoted fitness—he once wrote a high school track coach seeking advice from "the master" that "too many boys stay in their automobile seats when walking would improve their leg strength"—he, like most track coaches of his era, didn't believe in lifting weights. The thinking was that an athlete would become "muscle-bound" and his performance would be hindered. Crane worked with weights without Hutsell's knowledge. "I knew Crane was spending much of his time in the weight room. I never told Coach. I stayed out of it. I didn't want to get caught in the middle between Hutsell and Crane. But Crane and I would laugh about his secret weightlifting sessions. Weight training was a big part of Crane's success."

Two other conference champions on the third-place 1960 team were New Jersey native, Joe Leichtnam, a football player, who won the javelin, and Jimmy Morrow, also a scholarship football player, who placed first in the 100-yard dash.

Several performers stood out on the 1961 SEC conference championship team and the 1962 third-place team. Jim Dozier won the mile, placed second in the 800, and ran a leg on the third-place mile relay team. Dozier had always wanted to play college basketball but received no scholarship offers. However, Auburn offered him one of its scarce track scholarships. Because Dozier's father wanted him to attend Auburn, he accepted. Rosen remembers Dozier as "one of the best distance runners ever to compete for Auburn. He ran a 4:14 mile, but if we had used the training methods we use now he could have been an NCAA champion." Dozier, usually one of the hardest-working athletes on the team, was working out one day with teammate Paul Krebs when Hutsell instructed both runners to run a course outside the stadium. Rosen tells what happened next. "Coach Hutsell and I climbed the stadium steps to the top to watch Dozier and Krebs do the workout. When we got to the top and looked out we saw both of them lying under a tree looking like they didn't have a care in the world. I heard Coach Hutsell yell, 'What the hell!' I never saw him so mad. He ran down the stadium steps and almost tripped and broke his neck."

The 1963 second-place team featured several football players. Most prominent among them was fullback Tucker Fredrickson, who would be the 1965 SEC football player of the year. He placed fourth in the shot put. Fredrickson weighed 210 pounds and stood six feet two but was smaller than most of the other shot putters. He made up for his lack of size with amazing quickness and agility in the shot ring. Fredrickson's football accomplishments were extraordinary. He played two ways, averaging 4.4 yards per carry as a fullback and leading the defense in interceptions as a safety. He won the Jacobs Award as the best blocking back in the Southeastern

Conference. In 1964, he was a runner-up for the Heisman Trophy, and he was drafted by the New York Giants in 1965. He remembers his track days at Auburn fondly. "The reason I threw the shot was to avoid spring football practice. I finally got smart in my junior year and tried to find ways to avoid football practice. Football practices then were brutal, a matter of survival of the fittest. Not like today. I'll always appreciate coaches Hutsell and Rosen for getting me out of football practice!"

Gary Ray dominated the sprints in 1963, winning the 100-yard dash in 9.3 seconds and the 200-yard dash in 21.0. Ray, a scholarship football player, was dubbed "the fastest white guy in the South," by Benny Marshall, sportswriter for the *Birmingham News*. The reason football players were so central to the success of Southern college track teams in the 1950s and '60s was two-fold: segregation and scholarships—black athletes were not recruited, and the fastest white athletes played football because of the availability of scholarships. Ray was a good example; he earned All American honors and eventually placed sixth in the 1963 NCAA meet.

Hutsell would reach the mandatory retirement age of 70 in September 1963. He wasn't happy about it; he was ill-suited for leisure, his health was excellent, and he still had the energy and drive to do his job. The 1963 team, his last, won all four of their dual meets, defeating Georgia, Alabama, Florida, and Georgia Tech, in that order, and finished third in the SEC championship meet behind LSU and Mississippi State.

When Hutsell announced his retirement, bringing to an end a 42-year run as head track and field coach, many of his former athletes began planning a surprise celebration for their esteemed mentor. The final track meet of the season, a dual meet against Alabama, was selected as the occasion. Hutsell's former athletes pooled money to present him with a new car, a 1963 Oldsmobile. The car was driven onto the track to surprise the coach. "Coach Hutsell was fanatical about the care of the track. So, all of a sudden they drove that big Oldsmobile on the track and headed right for Coach. As soon as he saw the car, he ran full speed at it, screaming at the top of his voice to get that 'blasted thing' off the track. He didn't realize it was a gift for him. That was Coach Hutsell."

Rosen expected to be appointed head coach, but months passed and he wasn't offered the position. He didn't lobby for the job but waited patiently. Nor did he discuss the job with Hutsell. He thought Hutsell would be unwilling to go out on a limb and recommend him for fear of being held responsible if Rosen's hire didn't work out. Rosen told Joan [he had married Joan Kinstler in 1957; see Chapter 4] that if he didn't get the head coaching position he would continue his teaching for the year and then begin looking for other coaching jobs. Rosen felt strongly about two things: he would not remain at Auburn as an instructor in the physical education department, or serve as assistant coach to someone else.

As the weeks passed, Rosen grew concerned that his Jewishness was working against him. There was some evidence to support his fear. Hawthorne Wesley remembers talk around the athletic department by some of the coaches questioning whether a New York Jew could recruit Southern athletes or convince potential walk-ons to come out for the team. Rosen himself recalls: "Well, you know I was still an outsider, a Jewish guy from Brooklyn. So they may have been hesitant about bringing in this Yankee. I don't think there were any other Northerners on the staff at that time."

ROSEN'S THREE-MONTH WAIT FINALLY came to an end with a phone call from Jeff Beard, Auburn's athletic director. "When the call came I wasn't sure if it was going to be good news or bad." It was good. In August 1963, Mel Rosen, a Jew from Brooklyn, was named head track coach of Auburn University, only the second head track coach in Auburn's history. His salary for the 1964 season would be $6,600, and he didn't try to negotiate for more. "The money was the farthest thing from my mind. In fact, I never signed a contract, never saw one. Beard just told me the salary, and I took him at his word."

Rosen didn't know at the time that Beard had "lowballed" his salary. The original budget for the position had been $10,000. But Beard decided on a lesser salary with the athletic department funding half and the physical education department paying half. Notwithstanding one of the two preconditions he had declared to himself about staying at Auburn—not to continue teaching in the physical education department—Rosen thus was required to carry a teaching load of four classes along with coaching. It was an unusual arrangement; most head coaches weren't required to teach that much, if at all.

Rosen also learned later that the coaching position was first offered to Fred Carley, a Hutsell favorite who ran for Auburn from 1946 to 1948, won the SEC championship in the mile for three years, and was named an All American. He ranked sixth in the country in the mile in his senior year. Carley had received the first full track scholarship awarded by Hutsell in 1946 and later served as his graduate assistant for two years. While Hutsell hadn't lobbied for Rosen, he must have pushed behind the scenes for his protégé, Carley. Hutsell and Beard were close friends. Beard's older brother Percy had run for Auburn and placed second in the high hurdles in 1932 Olympics, and Beard himself had thrown the discus for Hutsell from 1930 to 1932. Beard certainly would have consulted Hutsell for a recommendation for Hutsell's replacement.

Carley recalls Beard's phone call offering him the job. "He asked me if I wanted the head coaching position. Beard said I'd be perfect to lead the team. He told me the salary, around $10,000 per year. The figure surprised me. I was making twice that amount in Mobile working as an engineer. I turned down the offer. But it wasn't just the money. Auburn was not in a good position. They couldn't compete with programs like Tennessee and LSU, schools that had many more scholarships to offer."

Only after Carley turned it down was Rosen offered the position. In fact, Beard still wasn't convinced Rosen was the right man for the job and considered him a transitional coach. In a September 1963 memo, he wrote to W. T. Ingram, AU business manager: "I feel we can get by with [Rosen] on a trial basis under this arrangement." He obviously was prepared to replace Rosen should he not find early success.

Rosen was stoic. "I guess they needed a lot of time to think it over before giving a Yankee the job," he commented years later to sportswriter Elliot Denman.[8]

An interesting question is why Beard was so hesitant to offer Rosen the job, even after Carley, his first choice, had turned it down. After all, Rosen had served successfully and loyally as Hutsell's assistant for eight years. Carley sheds some light on the matter. "I was surprised Auburn was hesitant to offer Rosen the job. He was a good coach and a fast learner. But I heard rumors that some in the athletic department were concerned about Rosen being Jewish. I don't know if that is true, but yes, there were rumors at the time."

After Auburn announced Rosen as the new head coach, a sportswriter from Birmingham called him. The sportswriter asked Rosen if he had been a student at Auburn. "No." He then asked Rosen if he was a graduate of Georgia or Tennessee. Again, "No." Next the writer asked what church he attended. Rosen, noting the ever-increasing frustration of the writer, said "I'm Jewish. I go to the synagogue." There was silence at the other end of the line. Then, impatiently, the writer said, "I think I have enough. I need to go," and hung up the phone.

THE THREE MONTHS AUBURN took to name Rosen head coach added to the general concern around the campus as to whether he could successfully replace Hutsell. Auburn's student newspaper, the *Auburn Plainsman*, commented on Hutsell's retirement by saying Hutsell's absence "will leave a space so big in Tiger Sports that there seems no way that it can be filled. Coach Hutsell is to Auburn as George Washington is to America."[9]

There were others who understood the challenges Rosen faced as the coach who replaced Hutsell. James E. Foy, Auburn's dean of students, wrote Rosen in October 1963, "May I take this opportunity to extend sincere congratulations and best wishes to you on your selection as track coach. I know that at this point you are awed by the prospect of following a man of Coach Hutsell's dimensions."[10]

F. X. Cretzmeyer, Rosen's former mentor from the University of Iowa, wrote a congratulatory note, which included this vote of confidence, "Don't worry, you'll always have Wilbur Hutsell close by to help you."[11] This sentiment was shared by the *Atlanta Journal*. After announcing his promotion, the sportswriter mused that fortunately Rosen's old mentor "will still be around for sage advice."[12] However Hutsell knew Rosen was a perfectionist with the ability and drive to be successful. "I don't think there really was much pressure on Mel when he took over," Hutsell commented to the *Plainsman*. "Of course, he was anxious to make good. But any pressure was from the inside out. That pressure will be the same 40 years from now, because Mel wants to do a good job. He's not satisfied with doing anything in an inferior manner."[13]

ROSEN DELIGHTED IN THE fact that Hutsell was a beloved figure at Auburn. He considered Hutsell his friend and mentor. He was not intimidated replacing the man with the ever-present cigar.

Rosen's first official act as head coach was to invite Hutsell to serve as his unpaid assistant. "I knew he wanted to stay involved, and I could use his skills and experience. After all, we were friends." Hutsell accepted immediately. His whole world had been Auburn athletics, and Rosen gave him the opportunity to stay involved.

The complete role reversal for the two men could have caused problems, but there were none; each understood his new role. "Coach Hutsell didn't want to retire. Track was his whole life. He adapted well to the assistant's role. He wanted to work with the hurdlers and throwers. Coach Hutsell was the perfect assistant. Never once did he come to me and question any decision I made as head coach. He was a loyal assistant as I was a loyal assistant to him. We had an excellent working relationship."

When Hutsell's health and eyesight began failing some years later, Rosen assigned a graduate assistant to drive Hutsell to the track and back home after practice. This allowed Hutsell to remain actively involved with the team. Including the 17 years Hutsell would serve as Rosen's unpaid assistant, he served Auburn University's athletic department for an incredible 56 years. Hutsell was inducted into the National Track and Field Hall of Fame in 1975 when he turned 84.

The coaching change from Hutsell to Rosen was more than just a change in leadership. It represented a philosophical change in the program as well. No other two men could have symbolized more the conflicting attitudes and philosophies of the Old and New South. While Rosen's hiring, despite his being a Northern Jew, signaled that things were changing at Auburn, integrating Auburn's sports programs still would come slowly. "I knew Auburn would not recruit African American athletes until Alabama did so. Auburn sometimes seemed to follow suit regarding Alabama."

As Rosen took over the daily coaching responsibilities, he focused on how Auburn could compete with Tennessee, Florida, and Louisiana State University, schools that were moving toward recruiting black athletes. Rosen understood Auburn could not be successful in the competitive SEC, let alone on a national level, without African American athletes. He also understood that without an adequate number of scholarships, he could not recruit blue-chip athletes. The days of winning conference championships with four scholarships were coming to an end. He needed to find a way to guide Auburn's program to national prominence, to be able to compete with schools from the Big Ten and Pac Ten, the two conferences with the strongest track and field programs, schools with long, successful histories recruiting black athletes.

Rosen wanted to increase the visibility of the track program by expanding the schedule. He planned to schedule meets against teams from the Big Ten and the Pac Ten to increase the team's visibility. Rosen knew too well the lack of interest in track in Alabama. Hutsell had once told Rosen that after Percy Beard won his silver medal in the high hurdles at the 1932 Olympics, "his hometown paper, the *Greensboro Watchman*, said 'Percy Beard has just returned home after competing in a footrace.' Coach Hutsell loved telling that story."

While interest in track and field would eventually grow, in the 1950s and '60s most Alabamians took interest in the sport only during the Olympic years. Never mind that Alabama was the state that produced Jesse Owens, whom the Associated Press ranked among the 10 top athletes of the century.[14] Owen's four gold medals in Berlin in 1936 had made him an international star. Even Southern newspapers, which normally ignored black athletes, carried pictures and stories about Owens.[15] Yet Owens's sport, track and field, could not even draw a crowd to meets in Alabama.

Rosen understood that Auburn could not compete successfully under such circumstances. Unlike Hutsell, who didn't like giving scholarships and never lobbied for more, Rosen met with Beard to ask for more scholarships. Beard refused. Even though Beard himself was a former Auburn track athlete, he put little money into the track program or, for that matter, any of the spring sports. He felt a track coach needed only four scholarships to compete successfully—one each for a sprinter, a jumper, a thrower, and a distance runner.

The dominance of football and basketball meant that Auburn lacked the resources to adequately support spring sports. In fact, Beard, who had been athletic director since 1951, spent time planning how to cut expenditures. Rosen told Beard during a budget meeting in 1964 that he wanted to buy a trowel to put down sand in the long jump pit. Beard asked Rosen the cost of the tool. Rosen replied that $7.95 would take care of it. He remembers Beard's response: "What happened to Bradberry? Did he break his hand?" Buck Bradberry was an assistant football coach and for years was an official for the long jump event. He had always used his hand to smooth the sand in front of the take-off board after each athlete completed his jump. "He just squeezed money until it started dripping water. It made it difficult to move the track program in a positive direction."

Nevertheless, Rosen felt that if Hutsell had asked, Beard would have delivered more scholarships for the track team. But Hutsell was more interested in the student athlete, the walk-ons from Alabama. He liked to watch them progress. Beard, meanwhile, "was mostly concerned about the football team and its success."

The dearth of track scholarships required Rosen to choose carefully athletes who could compete in multiple events. In 1962, Rosen was recruiting quarter-miler and long jumper Wade Currington from Montgomery and Bill Sellmer, a quarter-miler from Atlanta. However, Hutsell wouldn't approve signing both athletes, even though two scholarships were available. Hutsell didn't like awarding scholarships even if he had them to give. Rosen ended up signing Currington because he felt he was a better bargain; he could compete in two events. It was a good decision. Currington placed in both events in three conference championships and, in his senior year, won the long jump in the 1966 SEC conference championships.

Finally, there was the race barrier, a challenge that would be even more difficult for Rosen to solve than the paucity of scholarships. He knew Auburn would move slowly in admitting African American students and even more slowly desegregating their athletic programs. Rosen figured the football team would likely be the first sport to integrate at Auburn because of Coach Jordan's influence and the pressure for the football team to win. Rosen understood that as long as he didn't have the necessary scholarships and until Auburn could recruit African American athletes, Auburn wasn't going to be a consistent winner in the SEC, let alone be a national power.

He had to change the prevailing philosophy of what constituted a successful track program. "The measure of success for the head track coach in those years was to keep the program clean, don't get into any trouble with the NCAA, and just have a presentable team. But I wanted more than that. I didn't want to settle for mediocrity, even if that was enough for job security."

Rosen wanted to put Auburn track on the national stage. Rosen, after eight years serving as Hutsell's assistant, had a plan of his own.

4

One Track Mind

"I was loyal to individuals, not causes."

Rosen was a liberal Democrat, as most Jews from New York City of that era were, but after leaving Brooklyn he mostly avoided political discussions with his friends, fellow coaches, and athletes. Rosen wasn't an activist and didn't join political causes. That's not to say he didn't have views on the events of the time, but he was careful about expressing them. With each passing year as Hutsell's assistant, he grew more impatient with Auburn's dearth of black athletes and Hutsell's failure to push for recruiting them. While he supported the *Brown* decision and was not completely comfortable living in the segregated South, he never discussed these issues with his colleagues or friends. Rosen learned that getting along sometimes meant keeping your political views to yourself, particularly if you were an outsider. "I didn't make my Jewishness or my politics an issue. I am not even sure those from small Alabama towns would have known I'm Jewish. And that was fine with me."

Many of the athletic coaches and instructors in the physical education department were from small towns and had had little interaction with Jews. Rosen shared an office with Paul Nix, the head baseball coach; Cary "Shot" Senn, an assistant football coach; and Dick McGowen, Auburn's football recruiter. Conversations among the men most days revolved around sports. However, after having shared an office with Rosen for several years, one day Nix stopped in front of his desk and with a quizzical look asked, "Rosen, are you Jewish?"

"I was a little surprised, but I just said, 'Yes, Paul, I'm Jewish.' I didn't know what else to say. Nix just looked at me a little uncomfortably and, shaking his head, finally said, 'I didn't know that.' Before he walked away I said, 'What, you want me to wear a sign around my neck advertising the fact?' He just turned and walked back to his desk. After that we never had another conversation about religion, which was fine with me. But there seemed to be a discomfort between us after that."

Rosen wanted to fit in with the general community as well as the small local Jewish community. As historian Lee Weissbach has written, assimilation of Jews into the mainstream American culture occurred more rapidly in the South, particularly in small towns in the 1940s and '50s, "as no critical mass remained in the small-town environment to allow for the survival of any sort of religiously observant lifestyle or intensively ethnic Jewish subcommunity."[1] That was certainly the case in Auburn. "Most of the Jews living in Auburn and Opelika owned businesses and were blended into the general community. These families had lived in the South for many years and had strong Southern identities and ties to the community. Auburn was an easy place to adapt to. The people were friendly and accepting."

Rosen began his career in Auburn at a time when anti-Semitism was on the wane in most parts of the country. However, notwithstanding the above-noted assimilation of individual Jews in small towns like Auburn and Opelika, the reality was that "the South was the most anti-Semitic region in the country."[2] In fact, "approximately 10 percent of bombings in the South between 1954–59 targeted Jewish concerns: synagogues, Jewish community centers, rabbis' houses."[3] In an 11-month period between 1957–58, there were four such attacks. In November 1957 in Charlotte, North Carolina, a package of explosives was found against the rear wall of Temple Beth-el. Four months later there was an attempted bombing of Temple Emanuel in Gastonia, North Carolina. The following month an explosion tore through the school annex of Miami's Orthodox Temple Beth-el. One month later dynamite was planted outside the conservative Beth-el synagogue in Birmingham, Alabama; fortunately, the fuse burned out before detonation. These bombings were motivated not only by anti-Semitism but also because of Jewish support for integration.

Rosen was aware of these bombings, particularly the attempt in Birmingham, but he didn't have a close group of Jewish friends and colleagues to discuss them with. Auburn wasn't exactly Brooklyn, with its array of Jewish people and institutions. In the mid-1950s, Jews were only about 265,000 of the approximately 40 million people residing in the South.[4] Only 8,500 Jews were in Alabama, with the greatest number living in Birmingham, Montgomery, and Mobile. The Auburn/Opelika area was the type of isolated Jewish community described by Weissbach. The closest synagogues were in Columbus, Georgia, about 45 minutes away, and Montgomery, about an hour away. Steve Whitfield argues the small Southern town "has imposed huge if not insuperable difficulties in sustaining the dynamics of Yiddishkeit."[5]

Yet there was a small, but cohesive Jewish community in Auburn/ Opelika. Henry Stern, a German refugee who came to Opelika in 1937 from Westheim-Westfalen when he was seven, remembers 10 to 15 Jewish families living in the area. Most of the breadwinners owned small businesses and a few were professors at the university. Many of the families had established close, personal relations with their white Christian neighbors. It was important for them to fit into the community; livelihoods depended on positive, stable relationships with Gentiles. The business community in Auburn and Opelika accepted Jewish families and Jewish-owned businesses. Stern recalls no overt acts of anti-Semitism. In fact, Stern, and several other Jewish business owners were actively involved in community organizations, thus fostering positive relationships with the non-Jewish community. Stern said, "We were paying our civic rent to a community that accepted us."

In the mid 1950s, Rabbi Eugene Blachschleger, the rabbi at Montgomery's Temple Beth-Or from 1933 to 1965, traveled to Auburn/Opelika once a month to lead religious services, usually on a Thursday evening. Stern remembers picking up Rabbi Blachschleger from the train station in the late afternoon and taking him to the Auburn University Student Union where services were usually held.

Rabbi Blachschleger would spend the night at the home of one of the families and leave by train the next morning. Stern remembers these visits fondly. "Rabbi Blachschleger arrived on the train from Montgomery at 4 p.m. He always got off the train carrying a big satchel filled with corned beef, salami, and Jewish rye bread. He conducted a short service, mostly a discussion on Jewish topics of interest. There were usually five or six university students, and 10 to 15 families."

Rosen also remembers Blachschleger's visits. "Rabbi Blachschleger was a good rabbi, he gave interesting and thoughtful sermons, and, most importantly, he'd bring corned-beef sandwiches for everyone. We couldn't wait for his talk to end so we could get to the corned beef in his satchel. I stopped attending as there were no young women my age to meet. But I missed those corned beef sandwiches."

As ROSEN SETTLED INTO Auburn in 1955–56, he had his mind on more than just work. He had chosen to leave Brooklyn, but he was homesick. He missed the warmth of his Brooklyn home and his Jewish friends who were almost like extended family. Rosen also wanted to get married and have a family. He wanted to provide a different family life for his children than he had growing up without a father. After all, he was already 27 years old and felt it was time to settle down, a sentiment shared by Mollie. She still had the dream of her son coming back to Brooklyn and beginning a family and helping out with the bills. She didn't hesitate to try to persuade her son to come home and marry a "nice Jewish girl."

Meanwhile, he had quickly discovered that living in places like Iowa City, Fort Benning, and Auburn severely limited his chances of meeting eligible Jewish women. So he was resigned to the fact that he would probably marry a Gentile girl. And if that happened, he worried how he would break such news to Mollie. "My mother felt no girl was good enough for 'her Melvin.' But if I married a non-Jewish girl, it would have caused even more trouble. It wouldn't have been a good scene."

In fact, Rosen had gotten engaged twice in the mid-1950s. He courted a young woman from Clarinda, Iowa, whom he met during graduate school. Within a few weeks of their first date, Rosen gave her an engagement ring; the same ring Leo had given Mollie in 1926. Rosen felt he and the girl were well-matched—she was pretty, vivacious, and had a good sense of humor, traits Rosen liked. The relationship progressed quickly until she brought Rosen home to meet her parents. As soon as they heard the name Rosen and his Brooklyn accent, he "felt the chill in the air." The evening was a disaster. Her parents openly voiced their objections to the engagement. It was clear to Rosen they wouldn't stand for their daughter marrying a Jew, particularly one from New York. Rosen realized on the spot that his relationship with the young woman would never withstand her parents' disapproval. The engagement was soon called off.

Within the year, on one of Rosen's visits home, he met a young woman from Brooklyn whose father owned a successful shoe store in Manhattan. Rosen had great expectations for the romance as she was Jewish and came from a well-to-do family, facts that would please Mollie. In just a few weeks Rosen was again engaged. Unfortunately, while Rosen got along famously with her parents, his relationship with the young woman waned considerably after he returned to Fort Benning. The young woman wasn't interested in moving South, nor did she have the patience to wait for Rosen to finish his service obligation. Just a few weeks after Rosen left New York, she began seeing someone else, and the engagement was called off.

Rosen took these personal setbacks in stride. "Each engagement was like running a race, and unfortunately I came in second. But I wasn't upset. I just prepared for the next one." His poise, maturity, and, importantly, sense of humor had grown considerably in the nine years he spent at the University of Iowa and Fort Benning. He learned to use his sense of humor to his advantage, to deflect problems with colleagues and athletes and keep setbacks in perspective. This personality trait, the ability to not overreact to setbacks and to see the humorous side of events, would serve Rosen well throughout his coaching career.

In the summer of 1956, Rosen went home to Brooklyn to visit his mother. He and several of his old high school friends rented a house on Fire Island, a resort then visited mostly by Jews from New York City. On Rosen's first night there, Shelly Bacher, a friend from his Brighton Beach days, introduced him to Joan Kinstler, a girl Shelly had been going out with while on vacation. As soon as Rosen met Joan, he knew "she was the one." He began planning how to replace his friend Bacher, and only shortly after their introduction, Rosen began his courtship of Joan. It was not, however, love at first sight for Joan. A graduate of Julia Richmond High School in Manhattan, Joan had never considered attending college and began working right out of high school. Now 25 years old, she was vacationing from her job at Gimbels Department Store. Joan recalls their first meeting on Labor Day 1956: "Mel was an educated man, but all the men I went out with were educated. I remember him talking about his coaching and teaching job at Auburn, but that didn't mean much to me. He asked me if I liked track. I told him I had once been to a track meet at Madison Square Garden. I think that impressed him, but to this day I can't tell you why in the world I went to that track meet." Joan didn't know it then, but attending many more track meets was in her future.

After the Fire Island weekend, Rosen continued his courtship of Joan in the city. They spent every minute together for the next two weeks until Rosen had to return to Auburn. For the next three months, Rosen instituted an old-fashioned courtship, with daily correspondence and telephone calls to Joan. It was a successful campaign.

Joan came to Auburn to visit Rosen for Thanksgiving 1956. They attended the Auburn-Florida State football game. Joan loved the activities and the college sports atmosphere. She was attracted to the enthusiasm of the college students. Even the fact that immediately after the game Auburn became a ghost town, as students returned home for Thanksgiving break, didn't dissuade Joan. She was beginning to think that the "Brooklyn transplant" was someone she could love. "The more I spent time with Mel," Joan recalls, "the more I realized he was someone I enjoyed being with. Living in the South was not something that I worried about. I got a strong feeling Mel would be a good husband and father."

Rosen proposed to Joan Thanksgiving weekend. Cautious after the demise of his last two engagements, Rosen didn't want Joan to get away, and he pressed her to set the wedding date quickly, during Christmas break. But Joan insisted plans couldn't be made that quickly, and their wedding was set for January 1957. Rosen returned to New York in December and brought Joan home to meet his mother. Mollie, naturally, didn't like Joan. In Mollie's mind Joan wasn't good enough. "Well, that was my mother. My mother wouldn't have been impressed if I had brought home that nice Jewish girl, Elizabeth Taylor. The one thing Joan had going for her was she was Jewish, even though she wasn't religious, but neither was I. But it didn't matter what Mama thought. I never asked for her approval. I just said we were going to get married."

Joan Kinstler and Mel Rosen were married in New York City on January 20, 1957, at the Belmont Plaza Hotel in Manhattan. Rabbi Edward Klein of the Free Synagogue officiated. Despite Mollie's initial negative reaction to Joan, the wedding was a festive event.

Mollie was happy that her only son was finally getting married, and she hung onto the hope he and Joan would move back to Brooklyn. Of course, that wasn't going to happen, both because of Rosen's work and because Joan had no interest in moving close to Mollie. She and Mollie never developed a close relationship.

From early adulthood, Rosen always gave his mother financial support. However, financial security had come too late in Mollie's life for her to fully enjoy it. She never shed the insecurities and anxiety of trying to earn enough for her and Mel during the years after Leo died. Mollie's life was also difficult because she never fully assimilated; except with her close circle of Jewish friends in Brighton Beach, she always felt the outsider. Rosen said, "I don't think my mother ever understood what I did for a living. I would send her newspaper clippings, but she was from the Old Country. It was a big disappointment to me that she never understood." While Mollie had come to appreciate American culture and all it had given her and Mel, she never quite fit in.

Rosen would receive word his mother was in the hospital while he was preparing the Auburn track team for the 1966 season. Mollie was suffering from congestive heart failure, a condition from which she would never fully recover. Rosen would see his mother for the last time in March 1967.

THE NEWLYWED ROSENS' FIRST residence was a second-floor, three-room apartment at 118 Gay Street in Auburn. Rosen had selected the apartment primarily for its location: Joan hadn't yet learned to drive, and she needed access to shopping. The first morning Rosen left for work, he told Joan where the A&P was located and said he'd be home for lunch. "I'd never seen a place like Auburn before," Joan recalls. "I was a city girl. The first thing people asked me was where I was from and what church I belonged to. I was taken aback and didn't know what to say." The transition from Manhattan to Auburn was abrupt, but Joan adapted quickly and settled in.

They suffered a calamity in March 1957 when they decided to take a belated honeymoon in Panama City, Florida. On the drive down, a dog ran onto the highway, and Rosen swerved to avoid hitting it and lost control of the car, which rolled over several times before coming to rest in a ditch. Rosen suffered four broken ribs, and Joan had two broken legs. They were rushed to the nearest hospital in Chipley, Florida. Because of complications from surgeries on her legs, Joan's parents insisted she come to New York for medical care. Joan convalesced at her parents' apartment on Riverside Drive for the next eight months. Rosen spent the summer with Joan, returning to Auburn in August while Joan remained in New York until November.

The car wreck had cancelled their Florida honeymoon, but Rosen recalls, "It was the time we spent in New York after the accident that we learned more about each other. We read, played cards, and other games. It was a nice time and made us closer. After that period of time, I knew I had made the right choice. We've been married now for a lifetime, so Joan must have come to the same conclusion."

After Joan recovered and returned to Auburn, she and Rosen began planning a family. Laurie was born December 24, 1959. Rosen took his responsibilities as a father seriously. He adjusted his work schedule so he could be home for dinner on the nights he was in town. He generally went back to his office after dinner. Fatherless most of his life, he was especially aware of the importance of being actively engaged. "I didn't want to be an absent father."

Karen, their second daughter, was born September 3, 1961. "Laurie weighed 4.5 lbs and Karen weighed 3.8 lbs. I figured if we had another one the child would be the weight of a pencil. We decided to stop at two children. People ask me if I am disappointed that I don't have a son. I never even thought about that. I am happy with the way things are."

MEL AND JOAN ATTEMPTED to provide a Jewish education for Karen and Laurie, not an easy task in Auburn in the 1960s. The Rosens enrolled their daughters in religious school at Temple Israel in Columbus, Georgia, about

30 miles from Auburn, and carpooled there with four other families. At the time, there was no Jewish school in Auburn. Even though Rosen and his wife weren't observant, they wanted their daughters to have knowledge of the Jewish Bible and to develop a Jewish identity, which easily could be lost living in a small, Southern town.

Karen and Laurie studied at Temple Israel for just a couple of years before they began to lose interest. The Rosens withdrew the girls from the school, ending Mel's connection to the synagogue in Columbus. The family had no religious links to the Jewish community until weekly religious services were established in an Auburn Presbyterian Church some years later. Auburn essentially lacked enough Jewish families and local institutions to maintain a Jewish way of life. One reason the Rosen family assimilated so easily into the rhythms of small-town Southern life was that although they claimed a Jewish identity, formal observance of their religion wasn't a major part of their lives.

MEL AND JOAN KEPT a small circle of friends, a few from the Jewish community, but mostly fellow coaches. Rosen credits Joan for making it possible for him to be successful. "Joan made it possible for me to keep the unusual hours required of all coaches. You have to remember, I was tied up with meets most weekends during the season. Without Joan's willingness to be flexible about my time with the family, I am not sure I could have been successful." Rosen was an involved parent during the off-season. But during the track season, according to Joan, "Mel had a one-track mind," and was often gone.

As soon as the girls were old enough, Joan began bringing them to the home track meets. They became fixtures at the track, often helping their father at practices and meets. The Rosens' social life revolved around track. Joan recalls: "Work always came first for Mel during track season. I wanted the girls to be involved with their dad as much as possible. Our dinner discussions were often about new track prospects Mel was recruiting and meets. Going to track meets was one way to keep the girls involved with their dad."

Karen, the youngest, would eventually become a well-known sportswriter and coauthored a book with her father titled, *Track and Field: The Running*

Events. When Laurie told her parents that she was getting married, her father's first response was to tell her not to set the wedding date during track season! Was Laurie surprised? "That was just my dad. Track is the love of his life."

DESPITE ROSEN'S HAPPY MARRIAGE and tranquil domestic life, the shadows of anti-Semitism and segregation still loomed. While Jews played a significant role in championing black civil rights, "when we speak of Jews involved in black-Jewish political partnerships during the civil rights era, Northern Jews generally come to mind."[6] Simply, "Jews in the South generally shied away from high-profile engagement with political issues."[7] For example, at the height of the civil rights movement Rabbi Richard Winograd, director of the University of Chicago Hillel, was one of 20 rabbis who marched with Dr. Martin Luther King to protest segregation in Birmingham in May 1963. "Local African American leaders hailed the rabbi as a man committed to high moral ideals, but the Jewish community opposed Winograd's effort and criticized him for his high-publicity venture."[8]

Historian Wayne Flynt colorfully assesses Southern whites and their attitudes toward anyone who came south to fight for integration: "With a chip on their shoulder as large as Cheaha Mountain, white Alabamians also disliked outsiders in general and Yankees in particular."[9]

Southern Jews had reason to be wary. Segregationists had identified Northern Jews as the source of all their problems, but Jews living in small Southern towns feared a white backlash should they be associated with the movement towards integration. In the South, Jewish merchants had often developed close relationships with the black community. Henry Stern remembers that many Jews living in the South were not happy about Northern Jews demonstrating for desegregation. "We didn't like to see Jews from the North coming down to our home and telling us how to live our lives."

Stern said that Jewish families living in Auburn and Opelika had good relations with both the white and black communities. "Black customers," he recalls, "knew when they entered a Jewish-owned business they would be treated fairly and with respect. They also knew they could haggle about the price with us. Jews knew hard times, what it means to be a minority. We could relate to them." Nonetheless, few Southern Jewish business owners pushed openly for desegregation. As well, with significant exceptions like Jacob Rothschild of Atlanta and Milton Grafman of Birmingham, few rabbis from the South took leadership roles in the struggle for civil rights. In response to Alabama Governor George Wallace's 1963 inaugural tirade for "segregation now, segregation tomorrow, segregation forever," Grafman wrote in the *Birmingham News*: "It is clear that a series of court decisions may soon bring about desegregation of certain schools and colleges in Alabama. Many sincere people oppose this change and are deeply troubled by it. As Southerners we understand this. We nevertheless feel that defiance is neither the right answer nor the solution."[10] However, many rabbis guiding congregations in the South, particularly those in smaller towns, were leery of jeopardizing their comfortable way of life in their communities and didn't take an active, public stance against desegregation.

RACE TO THE BOTTOM

(1964–1972)

"In seven years through hard work and determination I took an Auburn track team from fighting for first place in the conference to dead last."

As he walked into his office the day after being appointed head track coach in 1963, the 35-year-old Rosen knew the main reason he had the position was that Auburn had gotten him on the cheap, for just an additional $2,400 a year over his salary as an assistant. However, Rosen didn't care about the money. He was elated with his new opportunity. "I was feeling good because I had achieved my goal. But I knew you don't replace a legend. It's better to replace the coach who replaces the legend, because the first replacement most likely will get fired."

On the other hand, Rosen was not worried about getting fired. He had earned tenure as a professor in the physical education department in 1958, so if coaching at Auburn didn't work out, he could continue to teach while looking for another coaching job. He wouldn't want to, but he could. Most significantly, however, he believed in himself as a coach. He knew that no matter where he'd coached, his athletes had improved under his watchful eye. "I have always had confidence in my abilities. I knew I was limited on some of the [non-scholarship] talent I was going to have, but I always felt that I can make athletes that I am coaching as good as they can be." Rosen had good reason to be confident. He had matured and perfected his methods during his eight years as assistant coach. He understood the pressures he would face as head coach. He had learned from Hutsell, the master tacti-

Rosen, far right, with members of his first Auburn team, 1964.

cian, not to overwork the team. He now learned how to train an athlete to prepare him to give his peak performance at meet time.

Rosen motivated his athletes to pay attention to their technique during workouts. Technique and form running were the focus of the Hutsell-Rosen workouts. Years later, after Rosen was named head coach of the 1992 men's Olympic Track and Field Team, he received requests for his workouts from high school coaches from all over the country. Invariably these coaches were flabbergasted that the daily workouts Rosen developed for sprinters were not as rigorous as they had expected and placed such emphasis on form running. Rosen had also learned from Hutsell that requiring athletes to wear flats—running shoes without metal spikes—during all workouts significantly reduced the number of foot and leg injuries.

The usefulness of these training methods caught the eye of other coaches. Several years into Rosen's head coaching career, Willie Williams of the University of Arizona approached Rosen during a meet and said, "Mel, I have better sprinters than you but your sprinters are always on the track while mine are in the stands injured and watching the meet. What's your secret?"

"I told him that my philosophy was to do everything I could to avoid getting an athlete hurt. I followed this approach even as the Olympic coach."

Hawthorne Wesley recalls Rosen's emerging coaching style: "Many coaches have technical skills, that's important, of course, but Mel combined the technical knowledge with the interpersonal skills to motivate collegiate athletes. In some respects it was a surprise he was so successful because he was different than many of the coaches and most of us on the team, but his New York demeanor combined with his sense of humor worked; it worked very well."

Rosen, whose unfettered childhood was spent roaming the Jewish neighborhoods of Brooklyn, was a street fighter who tempered his single-minded toughness with his sense of humor. He was willing to battle as hard and as long as it took to be successful on the track. It was this fighting spirit, a quality shared by many first- and second-generation Jews, that his athletes saw and appreciated. Rosen knew almost instinctively that when you have the whistle, there is no such thing as small talk with your athletes; what you tell them carries weight. Rosen understood that it is the brief encounters during practices that lay the groundwork for motivation and success. According to author James Michener, "Coaches tend to be simplistic, conservative and dictatorial and the outstanding ones have these characteristics to a marked degree."[1] Rosen, however, was different. He was not dogmatic, was willing to listen to advice, and, like his mentor F. X. Cretzmeyer, routinely read research journals in physical education to keep up with the newest training methods. Throughout his career, Rosen was quick to change his coaching techniques if he saw evidence that other methods were superior.

In a congratulatory letter to Rosen after Auburn won an SEC conference indoor championship, Bill Arnsparger, former defensive coordinator for the Miami Dolphins, one-time head football coach at LSU, and former athletic director at the University of Florida, wrote that Rosen and the other great coaches he'd encountered all had something in common: the ability to focus on the important details that make for championship performance.[2]

Most importantly, Rosen inspired his athletes. They wanted to compete for him. Harvey Glance, the great Auburn sprinter and Olympic champion, said, "Coach Rosen was one of the reasons for my success as a runner. He treated all his athletes the same, whether you were world-class or not. The same rules applied to everyone, as I was to find out when I ran for him. Coach was respected, and the team listened to him. Mel was a great motivator. You always wanted to run your best for Mel."

SOON AFTER HIS APPOINTMENT, Rosen began putting his own stamp on the team with several bold moves. For one thing, he wanted to increase the public's awareness of track. Track was not embraced in many small towns in the rural South. According to Rosen, the South was "50 years behind the rest of the country in building track programs."[3]

In an interview, Rosen said, "Track coaches in the South have a harder job than those in the East and Midwest. The boys are much less developed in track skills in high schools here in the South." He spent considerable time teaching the fundamentals to many of his Southern athletes, particularly those coming from rural areas in Alabama. This was the only way to give them the necessary skills to compete in the SEC.

Rosen had been helping high school coaches across the South establish track programs. This effort was part of his long-term strategy to reestablish Auburn track. His efforts were beginning to pay off. In an interview Rosen discussed the growing popularity of track. "Track has come a long way in the 10 or 11 years that I've been down here. You can start with the high schools as one big reason for its popularity rise. They've put a lot more emphasis on track in the past few years; therefore college track has developed and is better and more competitive."[4]

Rosen also expanded Auburn's schedule. For 41 years Hutsell had scheduled four dual meets—including the Florida Relays, the Georgia AAU meet, and the SEC Conference Championships—for each outdoor season. Rosen felt this schedule, limited to a select group of teams, did not provide Auburn enough national exposure. Rosen added to the schedule the Penn Relays, the meet he often attended as a student at Lincoln High School. This meet, established in 1895, is the longest uninterrupted track meet in the country and is arguably the most prestigious annual track and field meet in the United States. Rosen knew that if Auburn could be successful at the Penn Relays, national attention would soon follow. "You have to understand 30,000 to 40,000 fans attended the Penn Relays. I wanted all of them to see the name Auburn, and when they saw it know Auburn had a track team and it was a good one." Because the Penn Relays also featured some of the best high school track and field performers in the country, a trip to Philadelphia allowed him to recruit at no added cost to Auburn.

Not everyone appreciated the scaling back of dual meets against Georgia Tech, Alabama, Georgia, and Florida. Jim Dozier, SEC champion in the mile in 1961 and 1962, felt these special long-time rivalries were an important Auburn institution. "I understood why coach Rosen wanted a national schedule, but the cutting back of our traditional dual meets took away some of the excitement. Lots of former athletes returned for these meets. The dual meets brought Auburn fans together. We lost something when Rosen scheduled mostly invitational meets."

In early 1964, Rosen added another innovation to the Auburn track program: weight training for the entire team, including sprinters. Aside from the throwers, lifting weights was not a traditional training activity for track athletes at that time. Sprinters particularly had avoided weight lifting during the season for fear the increased muscle bulk would slow them down. But in recent years, weight training was being touted as a new method to improve an athlete's speed and endurance.

Initially, some Auburn athletes were skeptical, but most became believers when their performances improved over the course of the 1964 season. Rosen: "I think establishing weight training was instrumental in developing our great sprinters. In the early 1960s, weight training was used primarily with throwers. It was Harvey Glance who really benefited from weight training. He was a leader in the weight room. His intensity set the standard for the rest of the team."

THE FOUR-SCHOLARSHIP LIMIT WAS the most debilitating obstacle for Auburn track to overcome if the program was to consistently compete for an SEC championship. Non-scholarship athletes had always been the foundation of the Auburn track and field program. Hutsell's success was in large measure due to his uncanny ability to recruit and coach non-scholarship athletes.

It wasn't unusual for Hutsell and Rosen to carry 50 to 60 athletes on the team, obviously reflecting the heavy reliance on non-scholarship athletes. They permitted an athlete to remain on the team as long as he came to practice and followed workouts, irrespective of his performance levels. Rosen had first seen this attitude from Bresnahan at Iowa, and he saw it again at Auburn. "Coach Hutsell never wanted to cut any athlete from the team. I continued this practice as head coach. I guess we could have coached only those athletes who scored points in meets, but I think we became better coaches by trying to help all athletes, regardless of their talent levels."

As Hutsell had, Rosen always kept an eye out for Auburn students who seemed to have track potential. In September 1964, he walked into the first meeting of his basic physical education class, his lecture notes as always secured snugly in a folder under his arm. Rosen prepared for his classes just as he did for track practices—every minute was accounted for. When he called roll on that day, he noticed freshman Tom Mitchell, and as the semester progressed, he noted Mitchell's potential as a jumper. Rosen acted quickly and persuaded Mitchell to try out for the track team. "Coach Rosen asked me to come out for the team because he saw I was pretty good in the long jump and the triple jump. And things just grew from there."[5] Unfortunately, Mitchell sat out much of his freshman year with a painful back injury. But in his sophomore year, Mitchell began scoring points in meets and living up to Rosen's expectations.

In 1928 Hutsell had begun a tradition that continues to this day, the Omicron Delta Kappa (ODK) Cake Race, an annual event where Auburn students complete in a two and a half mile race to win a cake freshly baked by one of the campus sororities. Hutsell's original goal for the race was to increase the awareness of track and field at Auburn. But Hutsell and then Rosen also used the race as an important recruiting opportunity. It wasn't unusual for Rosen to identify two or three potential athletes from the annual cake race. Glenn McWaters was one of the most successful examples. McWaters placed sixth in the 1963 cake race. The five runners who finished ahead of him were all on the cross-country team. Rosen collared McWaters after the race and invited him to come out for the track team. When McWaters asked for a scholarship, Rosen explained there were none to give, but if he joined the team and earned points he could receive a partial scholarship the following year. McWaters eventually placed fourth in the mile at the 1967 SEC championships.

However, a single on-campus event was a weak answer to the overall problem. Rosen knew that Auburn was steadily losing the recruiting war. During the 1964 season, Rosen met with athletic director Jeff Beard to ask for additional scholarships. He approached the meeting with the confidence that comes with being the new head coach. As he entered Beard's office he anticipated he would be successful. After all, Rosen was proud of his skills of persuasion, honed growing up in Brighton Beach. He knew how to use his Brooklyn wit to draw people to his side. But the meeting with Beard ended in failure. Beard, a former track star of the old school, felt that four scholarships were sufficient and any more was just extravagant. "As soon as I began I could see he wasn't going to budge. I should have known if he hadn't given his good friend Wilbur Hutsell additional scholarships, he wasn't going to give any to me. It was a disappointment. When I walked out of his office I didn't know how I could keep up with programs like Tennessee that gave up to 50 scholarships. The playing field wasn't level."

To compensate for the lack of scholarship money, Rosen told recruits that while there were no scholarships to award presently, if they performed well their freshman year he might be able to provide support in the form of a partial scholarship or a table job in the school cafeteria. He also touted the new, expanded track and field schedule as an inducement to come to Auburn.

Because there was no budget for coaches' travel, recruiting was mostly done by phone and correspondence. To strengthen recruiting efforts, Rosen turned to alumni for help. Rosen felt they could persuade parents to send their sons to Auburn University, despite the lack of financial support. Also, Beard had always worried that Rosen would have trouble recruiting Southern athletes. Rosen understood the concern: "I delegated some of the contacts to our former athletes as I'm not sure in those early years the boys we were recruiting wanted to hear a voice with a Brooklyn accent."

Hawthorne Wesley, who ran for Auburn from 1955 to 1957, sometimes helped with recruiting. His involvement was important, as he understood how to sell Auburn to an athlete and his parents. His gentlemanly manner and ability to convey that Auburn was "a special place" was often persuasive. For example, in 1971 he wrote to a prospective athlete extolling the benefits of an education at Auburn. It is clear that Wesley is also directing his comments to the recruit's family. "Our campus still retains the old fashion college atmosphere despite the fact that we have a nine-story building and an atomic reactor on campus. In troubled times our campus has been almost completely free of disturbances. We had absolutely no demonstrations when we integrated and since then subjects like the Vietnam War, coed freedom and social changes have been approached in a civilized manner."[6]

Rosen, a competitive recruiter, persuaded some athletes to come to Auburn without financial aid. "I told recruits that I would always be at practice for them. I wouldn't be traveling around the country neglecting them. And for the most part, I lived up to that standard."

Sometimes, however, non-scholarship athletes couldn't afford to continue their studies. One athlete wrote Rosen in 1967, ". . . I will not be able to run track this year. I am not financially able to come to Auburn because my dad has been on strike for 13 weeks."

These problems were to plague Rosen's teams until more scholarships were allotted in 1972.

NOTWITHSTANDING THE LACK OF scholarships that he and Hutsell had had to recruit with, Rosen's 1964 team, his first as head coach, was a powerhouse. The *Atlanta Journal* wrote that "Auburn has unprecedented strength in the pole vault, superior depth in the broad jump, and is phenomenal in the quarter-mile."[7] The team lived up to expectations by winning all of its dual meets and placing second in the SEC championships, just behind heavily favored Tennessee. Team captain Tom Mitchell placed first in the broad jump and second in the triple jump, just behind the winner, teammate Harvey Johnston. Sophomore Tom Christopher, nicknamed the "Flying Tiger," won the pole vault. He would become Rosen's first NCAA All American (of a total eventually reaching 143). In addition to these first-place finishes, Auburn showed its overall depth by scoring an impressive six second-place finishes. Among those, Jerry Smith stood out. He placed second in the 440-yard dash and helped the mile relay team place third.

Smith, a senior from Birmingham, was one of the leaders on the team. He had won the conference in the 440-yard dash in 1962 and in 1963 placed third in the event. He was also part of the mile relay team. His determination and unmatched work ethic impressed Rosen. The *Auburn Plainsman* described Smith as "the type of person who excels under pressure. He has a tremendous desire and the ability to take the type of punishment a star trackman must endure"[8] Smith's enthusiasm and capacity for hard work were contagious, making his teammates better. However, Smith was constantly pestering Rosen for more difficult workouts. He wanted to push himself to the limit during practice, while Rosen's philosophy was to undertrain to avoid injury. Smith wouldn't accept that reasoning and kept pestering Rosen for longer, more grueling workouts. One day Rosen gave Smith what he wanted. Two hours later, Rosen saw him on the ground exhausted and writhing in pain from leg cramps. Rosen, not wanting to miss his opportunity to make his point, walked up and asked, "Smith, was the workout hard enough for you?"

One of Rosen's goals was to take his best athletes to national meets, a practice that rarely happened during Hutsell's tenure. Rosen took sprinter and long jumper Bill McCormick and middle-distance runner Jerry Smith to the 1964 NCAA Eastern Regional Meet in Louisville. Rosen had high hopes for both. Smith placed third in the 600-yard dash. However, McCormick scratched in his first two attempts in the long jump. A distraught McCormick came running up to Rosen for advice and encouragement.

Rosen: "McCormick was beside himself after his second scratch. I told him to back up his approach about a foot and keep his eyes focused a couple of feet in front of the takeoff board and that would take care of the problem. Then he asked me if I thought he should wear his glasses when jumping. He had decided to put his glasses to the side so he would be lighter on takeoff. 'What?' I screamed. 'Are you crazy? Wear your glasses!' He scratched on his third attempt. So much for my sage advice."

At the end of the 1964 season, Gerald Rutberg, sports columnist for the *Auburn Plainsman*, summed up Rosen's first season: "Coach Rosen and his charges earn our congratulations for a job well done under a degree of pressure. It's not easy to take over the reigns from a coach who had produced 43 years of outstanding track and field achievements. Coach Rosen has only 42 years to go."[9]

Another interesting moment for Rosen during the 1964 season came during the Auburn vs. Chattanooga homecoming football game (Auburn won, 33 to 12). Rosen had been a football fan since his youth in Brooklyn. As head track coach, Rosen was given seats on the 50-yard line for this game. Sitting directly in front of Mel and Joan was Governor George Wallace and his entourage. Rosen and Wallace, both vocal fans, quickly became acquainted. Every time Auburn made a good play, Wallace would turn in his seat and say, "Mel, what did you think about that play!" Throughout the game, Rosen and Wallace chatted about the plays and strategy. Neither was hesitant to disagree with Coach Ralph "Shug" Jordan's strategy. Of course, Rosen, a liberal Democrat, had not voted for Wallace for governor; he was appalled by Wallace's opportunistic, race-baiting politics. "I didn't like his politics but he was a nice guy and an enthusiastic Auburn fan. He never criticized individual players. He was very different than what you saw on the television." It was as if Wallace instinctively knew that Rosen, a New York Jew, was not his political ally, but, ever the consummate politician, was trying to get Rosen's vote.

Early on as head coach, Rosen revealed his personal philosophy in two other telling if low-key ways.

Perhaps because he was the father of two daughters, he was keenly aware of the limited opportunities afforded to women in collegiate sports. He wanted to do something about that. In the fall of 1963, he established the first physical education class in track for women at Auburn. At that time men and women had separate physical education courses, and track classes were not available for women. Rosen saw no reason why women should not have the opportunity to participate in track. The *Auburn Plainsman* announced Rosen's decision to offer track classes for women: "Recently Auburn has made the sports page in many newspapers across the nation and not only because of football. Why else would Auburn be making the sports page right now? Because this year Auburn is trying an experiment with a new physical education class for girls track."[10] Teaching coeds to be more knowledgeable about track was a small initial step in Rosen's long-term plan to have a women's track and field team at Auburn. Rosen broke another gender barrier by appointing the first female manager in any sport at Auburn. Again, the *Auburn Plainsman* covered the story: "Mel Rosen made one of the big breakthroughs in modern Auburn sports history when he agreed to have Claire 'Jerry' Stalnaker as manager." Rosen: "The girl started calling me . . . and when I finally was able to talk with her, she said she was interested in helping manage the track team." At first Rosen tried to avoid her, not knowing how his team would react to having a female manager. But the young woman was persistent. "She asked me again if she could manage, and since she seemed so determined, I told her to come out." Opening up these opportunities demonstrated Rosen's intent on changing a system that didn't give women equal opportunities in athletics.

At about this same time, representatives of the Fellowship of Christian Athletes (FCA) visited Rosen, seeking his permission to recruit members during practices. The FCA was established in 1954 by several high-profile sports figures: Otto Graham, Carl Erskine, and Branch Rickey. FCA had a foothold in Auburn; for years it had been recruiting athletes from the football and baseball teams. Rosen denied FCA's request to recruit during track practices. "I just didn't think it was the right thing to do to let them talk to the athletes about a Christian organization. It wasn't because I'm Jewish. I worried that some of the kids would feel uncomfortable with their message. This was one of my easier decisions. I felt that they could meet with anyone they wanted after practice, away from the track. I just didn't want to sanction the meeting by allowing it during practice time." Some years later, when Rosen had established himself as one of the most successful coaches in the country, the FCA contacted him to give a speech at one of their national programs. He declined the invitation.

ROSEN HAD GREAT HOPES for the 1965 season. Sixteen lettermen were returning, and he thought pole vaulter Tom Christopher could win the conference championship. However, Christopher began having difficulty with his vaulting technique, causing him to stall at the top of his vault, often landing on the bar and barely making it into the pit, a potentially dangerous outcome. Rosen tried to increase Christopher's runway speed and improve his timing. But it was to no avail. Rosen went to Hutsell and asked him to try. Hutsell, who loved special coaching assignments, immediately went to work with Christopher. But in this instance, the result was disaster. "I was on the other side of the track, but I could see Hutsell instructing Christopher," Rosen recalls. "I thought to myself, problem solved, when all of a sudden I heard screaming coming from the pole vault pit. I ran over and found Christopher moaning and holding his ankle. He'd broken it. His spikes got caught in the mats in the pit. I looked over to Hutsell and all he said was, 'Well, I got him in the pit.' He then just walked away." The injury kept Christopher sidelined for the 1965 outdoor season.

In Christopher's absence, Auburn placed a disappointing fourth in the conference championships. One of the stars for Auburn was Bill Meadows, who placed first in the triple jump after almost not making the trip. Rosen had a minute-by-minute schedule for travel meets. His rule was that he wouldn't wait for anyone who was late for the team bus. When Meadows didn't show for the 8 a.m. departure, an angry Rosen directed the bus driver to stop at Meadows's fraternity house. Rosen went in to roust Meadows from bed. A few minutes later, Rosen and a tired Meadows came running out. "I would have left him but we needed the points. These decisions you make as a coach."

Auburn captured second place, behind Tennessee, in the 1966 SEC outdoor championships. The jumping events were Auburn's strength. Wade Currington won the long jump, Bill Meadows won the triple jump, and Tom Christopher, healthy again, won the pole vault and placed second in the high jump. Rosen believed that Christopher, who held the SEC pole vault record of 15' 6¾", was the best vaulter in the conference.

During the 1966 season, Rosen was involved in an intense recruiting war for Richmond Flowers, a football and track star from Montgomery. Flowers was the most sought-after high school athlete in the South. Auburn, Alabama, and Tennessee were pulling out all the stops to sign him. Rosen worked with football coach Shug Jordan trying to recruit Flowers to Auburn. Rosen: "We never had a chance to get him. Flowers's father [Alabama Attorney General Richmond Flowers Sr.] was planning to run for governor so the son didn't want to sign with either Auburn or Alabama so as not to alienate voters from either side. That's one reason why he chose Tennessee."

Rosen's success in his first three years as head coach had eliminated much of the doubt about him. The *Plainsman* praised Rosen's tenure. "Spring is here and spring naturally brings the spring sports to Auburn's flowering campus. At least one of these sports, track to be specific, is in full bloom, and Auburn's thinclads are running strong."[11]

However, despite his team's success, Rosen was concerned with the direction of the program. He felt difficult times were coming.

Tennessee won the conference championship again in 1967 while Auburn fell to forth. Auburn dominated the triple jump—Bill Meadows placed first, followed by teammates Mickey Jones and Jack Marsh. Marsh also won the long jump and Tom Christopher placed second in the pole vault. But Rosen was more concerned than ever about his ability to keep pace with Tennessee, Florida, and LSU. "We were falling further behind. We had excellent athletes but not enough of them because of the lack of scholarships. We just didn't have the depth to compete for the conference championship. Coach Chuck Rowe had done a great job convincing his athletic director at Tennessee to support them with scholarships."

While privately complaining to Beard about the lack of money for the track program, Rosen was diplomatic in his public statements. In an interview with the *Plainsman*, Rosen praised the athletic department. "The Athletic Department is certainly behind track whole heartedly. Coach Beard and Coach Jordan have always been interested in track, and I've had as much cooperation as I've hoped for since becoming head coach."

Behind the scenes, however, Rosen knew his program was falling further behind conference rivals.

ROSEN HAD NOW BEEN at Auburn for 11 years, but he was still considered an outsider by some of his fellow coaches. However, he was maturing as a coach. He was learning how to establish and maintain positive relationships with Beard and the rest of the athletic department. He worked at being fully accepted. He didn't discuss religion or politics, topics he considered off-limits. "You won't last long in coaching unless you have solid relationships with the athletic director and the university administration." Maintaining these relationships, however, can be difficult, particularly if you don't agree with policy set by your athletic director.

Jeff Beard mandated that athletes could not have long hair or wear beards. Coaches were expected to enforce the rule. Beard felt Auburn's fan base expected "Auburn men" to be clean-cut. In response to a reporter's question about his stringent grooming policy he said, "I am constantly getting complimentary letters from airlines, restaurants, and hotels on what a fine group of men Auburn has."[12] He goes on to say that spectators "like to see well-groomed people, the public pays a terrific price and demands a nice looking ball club." However, Rosen was ambivalent about enforcing grooming rules. George Cobb, an Auburn runner who had placed fourth in the 880 in the 1964 conference championships, was a graduate student in 1967. Even though the bearded Cobb was no longer a member of the team, Rosen allowed him to work out with them. One fall afternoon Beard happened to see a group of runners in the distance and noticed that one had a beard. Beard asked Rosen to come to his office with an explanation. "All of a sudden my athletic director is telling me that he saw one of my runners had a beard and reminded me of the rule. I told him we were in compliance with the rule but, because some of my runners were so slow, they began a race clean-shaven and finished with a beard. I am not so sure he saw the humor in that."

Rosen took Tom Christopher to the 1966 Millrose Games in New York. Christopher, cleared 15'6" and placed second. He also learned a lesson he wouldn't soon forget. On his first attempt at 15 feet, Christopher easily cleared the bar. He jumped up and began running out of the pit waving to the cheering crowd. Unfortunately, he ran into one of the standards. The collision knocked the bar off and Christopher, still in the pit, was credited with a miss. "From that point on I told all my jumpers to do their celebrating once they are out of the pit."

Auburn placed third in the 1968 conference meet, but they lost two of four dual meets, a rare occurrence for Auburn. Rosen's top performers were freshman Alvin Bresler, who placed second in the 120 high hurdles, just behind Tennessee star Richmond Flowers, long jumper Jack Marsh, and discus thrower Barry Erwin.

Alvin Bresler and his younger brother Milton were such versatile athletes and fierce competitors that Rosen would occasionally ask one of them to replace a teammate who was unable to run a particular race. In 1968, Robert Maxwell was scheduled to run a leg in the 1600-meter relay in Auburn's meet against Alabama in Tuscaloosa. This hotly contested meet came down to the relay to determine the winner. Rosen was at the starting line giving the team last-minute instructions when he saw that Maxwell was unusually nervous and was pacing back and forth and wringing his hands. The partisan fans were on their feet to cheer the home team. The officials called the runners to the starting line. There was a false start, which added to the tension. Just before the second start Maxwell, came up to Rosen and told him he couldn't run. It was too much pressure. Maxwell just walked away. In desperation, Rosen looked around for a replacement and found Alvin Bresler stretched out on the ground recovering from his effort in the just-finished intermediate hurdles. Rosen ran up to Bresler and told him to take Maxwell's place on the relay. Bresler protested that he was too tired and would hurt the team's chances if he ran. Rosen wouldn't take no for an answer. In spite of Bresler's effort, Auburn lost the relay and the meet.

Rosen: "I made it a rule after that to make myself scarce before every relay race until the gun goes off."

Foreshadowing coming change, the athlete who caused the biggest stir in the 1968 conference championship was Jim Green, a University of Kentucky football player who became the first African American to run track in the SEC. He won both the 100- and 220-yard dashes. The *Plainsman* described Green's impact this way: "Green, a Negro freshman . . . received the most outstanding individual trophy, and circulated a petition, along with [Tennessee's Richmond] Flowers, saying that athletes would boycott any future SEC meet at which the United States flag was not present."[13] The petition was a reaction to the SEC indoor meet held in Montgomery the year before when the only flag displayed was a Confederate battle flag.

In 1969, Auburn University completed construction of Memorial Coliseum, a new basketball arena. Auburn's first basketball game in the coliseum was January 11, 1969, against an LSU team featuring the great "Pistol" Pete Maravich. More than 11,000 fans watched Auburn win 90–71 (Maravich had 46 points). The new coliseum cost just over $6 million to complete and, according to former athletic director David Housel, "put Auburn on the map and helped us more successfully recruit in the SEC."

Most significant to Rosen about Memorial Coliseum was the indoor track that he had spent two years lobbying the administration to include. "I wanted to use the indoor track as a recruiting tool to tell athletes we could practice year-round. The track in the coliseum was the first good indoor track in the South."

Auburn's first indoor meet in Memorial Coliseum was against the University of Georgia, coached by Forest "Spec" Towns, who had been the 1936 Olympic champion in the high hurdles. Towns and Rosen had a competitive, prickly relationship, which added to the meet's tension. As the meet progressed, the long jumpers inadvertently kicked sand onto the smooth-surfaced track, making the footing precarious in one turn. In a couple of key races, Georgia runners couldn't negotiate the turn and fell. As a consequence, Auburn defeated Georgia. The loss enraged Towns and he confronted Rosen: "What the hell is going on here, Rosen? We got robbed." Rosen was never able to rehabilitate their relationship. "Towns was a good coach, but he had a gruff personality. I got a real kick out of beating him in our first meet in the coliseum."

Auburn finished a disappointing sixth as just six of its athletes scored points in the 1970 conference meet. Steve Richards from Columbus Georgia, ran his best race of the season and tied for second in the 120-yard hurdles, a pleasant surprise for Rosen. Milton Bresler placed third in the 440 hurdles, and Dave Parrish, a walk-on from Auburn, placed fourth in the triple jump. Donnie Fuller placed third in the 100-yard dash and fifth in the 220-yard dash.

A few days after the meet, Beard asked Rosen to come to his office. He complained that Fuller's school bills were significantly higher than those of anyone else on the team and said that Auburn couldn't support such an "expensive" athlete. Rosen replied that Fuller was an art major and was required to buy a lot of supplies for his classes. Beard, always worried about athletic department expenditures, told Rosen not to recruit art majors in the future.

"That was the low point. The lack of scholarships was killing our chances, then my athletic director was telling me I couldn't recruit art majors!"

The 1971 and 1972 seasons couldn't have been worse for Rosen's team as it continued a slide to the bottom of the conference. Auburn placed sixth in the 1971 championships. However, two important 1971 developments would prove to be the impetus for Auburn's climb back to the top.

First, Rosen hired Jerry Smith as his assistant. "I was surprised when Beard finally gave me permission to hire an assistant because I had been asking for help for years. I had no doubt Jerry was the right man to help us get back on top. He was a great coach and a fierce recruiter. Hiring Jerry was one of my best decisions as head coach." Rosen's selection of Smith showed his career-long ability to make good decisions during times of adversity. Smith would be a critical factor in Auburn's resurgence.

The other significant event was that Beard finally gave Rosen permission to recruit two African American athletes from Montgomery: Henry Orum, a long jumper, and Thomas Whatley, a sprinter. But only Orum and Whatley; no other African Americans. Rosen went to Montgomery and took both to dinner. Unfortunately, he was working with a tiny recruiting budget and could only afford to take them to McDonald's. "You should have seen their faces! They expected to be taken to a first-class restaurant. They both ended up at Alabama."

In the 1972 conference meet, Auburn scored only 19 points and finished eighth, last place, the worst conference finish in Auburn's history. Only three athletes scored points for Auburn: Milton Bresler took second in the 440-yard hurdles, Jerry Wooden placed third in the triple jump, and Steve Richards was fourth in the 120-yard hurdles.

"Our slide downward was a disaster. We weren't competitive with only four scholarships to give." Despite the team's collapse, Rosen wasn't being pressured to win by Athletic Director Jeff Beard. One reason Beard didn't support the track program was that his main interest was football. He put most of the department's resources into football, the only Auburn sport making money for the school. Because track wasn't considered important there was little pressure on Rosen to win. Also, Auburn's president, Dr.

Harry Philpott, was as concerned about running clean athletic programs as he was about winning. A last-place track team was of no great concern to him as long as the program was clean. Philpott told the *Plainsman*, "An intercollegiate program has to harmonize with the educational ends of the university. We all want to win; the desire to be a winner is a natural desire. I am not, however, an exponent of this philosophy that winning is everything."[14]

NOTWITHSTANDING AUBURN'S POOR SHOWING in the conference, Rosen's reputation was growing, as evidenced by his nomination for the 1972 Olympic coaching staff. He was known as a coach who worked effectively with athletes of all ability levels and who knew how to keep his athletes healthy. Rosen's experience working with walk-ons taught him to focus on an athlete's gradual improvement and not demand too much too soon. He understood the importance of an athlete's small improvements as the basis for bigger gains. A letter from a high school athlete illustrates Rosen's growing reputation: "I am not an outstanding trackman," the prospective Auburn student wrote, "but I'm sure if I was coached by you, I'd improve."[15]

Rosen felt his job was safe even after the eighth-place finish in 1972. "I knew the administration would be patient since I was running a clean program and my athletes were graduating." But Rosen wasn't interested only in job security. He wanted to win, and for the first time he began thinking about leaving Auburn for a school that supported its track program with scholarships and recruiting resources.

Then in May 1972, Athletic Director Jeff Beard unexpectedly announced his retirement. He had guided Auburn athletics for 22 successful years. The *Plainsman* summed up Beard's distinguished career: "Auburn athletic teams under Beard's guidance have racked up a stunning 1,336 victories against 613 losses and 18 ties." However, Beard was at odds with Dr. Philpott for raiding the athletic department's budget. The issue finally came to a head in 1972, and Beard, fed up with the situation, announced his retirement.

Lee Hayley became Auburn's athletic director three months later. Halyey, a native of Birmingham, had been captain of Auburn's 1956 football team and had served as assistant football coach under "Shug" Jordan for five seasons. He also was defensive coordinator under Coach Bill Dooley at the University of North Carolina for five years before his appointment as athletic director at Auburn.

Hayley moved quickly to put his own stamp on Auburn athletics. As soon as he arrived, he scheduled individual meetings with the coaches. When Rosen walked into Hayley's office, the first thing the new athletic director asked was "What will it take for you to win?" Rosen didn't hesitate: "Scholarships." Hayley increased track scholarships from four to eight.

And just like that, a new phase began in Rosen's tenure as head coach. "Finally we had an athlete director who was putting scholarship money into other programs besides football. It was the talk of the office for a long time."

Along with Hayley's arrival, expectations for Rosen to win increased dramatically. Because of the higher expectations, Rosen's recruiting efforts intensified. He understood that his success would be determined by his ability to recruit blue-chip athletes. Fortunately Jerry Smith was a tireless recruiter and would, in the course of the next few years, land some of the best high school athletes in the country.

Rosen remembers the intensity of their recruiting efforts. "During the day we were constantly on the phone to different high school and college coaches. At night we were talking to the prospects. Jerry traveled to different parts of the country to recruit, even to different parts of the world. The pressure was to always be on the move. You either did it that way or you weren't going to make it, particularly in the SEC."

The new pressure to win wasn't a problem for Rosen. He readily accepted the culture of winning. He wanted to match wits with the best coaches in the country. He was living his dream from his Brooklyn days. And if the opportunity to compete at the highest levels brought with it more pressure to win, so be it. Rosen embraced the challenge because he had a plan to put Auburn track and field back at the top of the conference. Central to that plan was the recruitment of African American athletes.

6

THE BURDEN OF
AUBURN HISTORY

"I never was out there about calling for integration. I wanted changes, but if I pushed the administration, I probably would have been fired. And what good would that have done?"

The South in 1964 was, as Hawthorne Wesley put it, going through "troubled times," a euphemism for the civil rights movement that was, step by inexorable step, dismantling the rigid system of Jim Crow segregation that had hobbled the region since the end of Reconstruction in the 19th century.

Though many had refused to accept it, Auburn University had been on an unalterable path toward integration since the *Brown* decision of 1954. As early as 1961, the *Auburn Plainsman* editorialized that racial desegregation "is inevitable and those who think it is not are either miserably stupid or living in self-delusion."

In Rosen's first year as head coach, Harold Franklin became the first African American student to enroll at Auburn University, on January 4, 1964, thus ending the land grant school's 108-year history of segregation. Auburn was one of the last SEC universities to desegregate, and it did so only after being forced by the federal courts.

Historically Auburn had denied applications from African Americans not overtly on the basis of color, but on the pretense that the prospective student's qualifications were inadequate. Auburn had tried to keep Franklin out by saying his undergraduate degree from Alabama State College (now University) was from an unaccredited school. Another method Auburn used to delay integration was to avoid applications from qualified blacks by setting them aside until enrollment was full, or by "withholding requested catalogues and admission forms."[1] These delaying tactics ultimately failed. Acting on a lawsuit filed by famed civil rights attorney Fred D. Gray of Tuskegee, U.S. District Court Judge Frank M. Johnson Jr. ultimately closed the door on Auburn's delaying tactics to keep Franklin from enrolling. Johnson played a crucial role in shaping civil rights law in Alabama; Martin Luther King Jr. described him as "the man who gave true meaning to the word *justice*."[2] Between 1955 and 1975, Johnson's rulings desegregated city buses in Montgomery and schools, parks, housing, and law enforcement throughout Alabama, eliminated the state's poll tax, reformed prisons and mental institutions, and authorized the 1965 Selma to Montgomery march, to name a few significant cases.

Auburn President Harry Philpott appealed Johnson's order to the U.S. Fifth Circuit Court of Appeals, which upheld the Montgomery judge. The inevitable had arrived. The *Auburn Plainsman*, typically a progressive voice, advised students, faculty, and staff "to go about their business as usual" on Franklin's first day.[3] Once he was attending classes the paper editorialized, "It is our opinion that Auburn stands a little taller. Most of us have every reason to be proud of our school and community."[4]

Auburn did have reason to feel good that it had "witnessed neither riots nor violence during desegregation."[5] Other flagship universities in the South had been less fortunate. White students at "the University of Alabama rioted for three days . . ." protesting the enrollment of two African American students. White students at the University of Georgia rioted for a week after two African American students enrolled in January 1961. Response to James Meridith's enrollment at the University of Mississippi in September 1962 was even "uglier." One reason for the relative calm at Auburn was that the administration and community leaders could draw on the experiences of those universities that had already desegregated. Rosen: "By the time he [Franklin] registered the atmosphere was calmer. The demagogic Wallace had focused his attention on blocking integration in public high schools across the state." Many credited Auburn President Ralph Draughon, who had succeeded Philpott, for skillfully leading Auburn "to a nonviolent solution to the racial problem it faced.[6]

ROSEN AND HIS COLLEAGUES in the shared athletic office weren't talking about the integration of Auburn. They didn't discuss politics. Rosen: "You have to remember the athletic offices were set apart from the rest of the University. It tended to isolate you from campus events. Also, coaches are generally not politically active. We have tunnel vision and focus on our sport."

The significance of Franklin's enrollment was obvious to all, even if it was only a first step. Rosen: "Auburn's desegregation was an important event—it should have occurred earlier. But it didn't change anything with the track team. We weren't given permission to recruit African American athletes. The sports programs at Auburn were still white-only."

Though African Americans were making gains in their fight for equality, racial problems remained and surfaced frequently. Preparing for a track meet in Mississippi, Rosen wrote to the Lamar Hotel in Meridian in April 1965 to reserve rooms. The hotel manager wrote back and told Rosen that "they would be honored" to have Auburn's track team as a guest at their hotel, however, "we do not receive guests other than of the white race."

Rosen: "We ended up staying there. Where else could we stay? In those years most of the motels in this part of the country were segregated. It was the times. I didn't like it at all, but I had to bring a track team to compete."

Ironically, as Rosen would discover, discrimination toward black athletes was not limited to the South, nor did it disappear quickly. In 1974, Rosen entered Clifford Outlin, a gifted athlete who was the first of a long line of great sprinters to compete for Auburn during Rosen's tenure, in the prestigious Millrose Games in New York City. Rosen's goal was to give his star sprinter experience competing in national meets against elite competition.

They had two extra days to spend in the city after the meet, so Rosen took Outlin to the New York City Athletic Club in Manhattan to schedule a workout. When they entered, the receptionist informed them that blacks were not allowed in the Athletic Club. Rosen: "I couldn't believe it. We come from Alabama, a place where you think you might face racism, but it is in New York City where we are confronted with it. I felt bad for Clifford."

Outlin remembers the incident well. He was embarrassed and thought that he and Rosen would just leave. But without a word Rosen took Outlin around the corner and entered the Athletic Club through a side door and went to the track and completed their workout. Outlin recalls, "When they wouldn't let us in Mel just took over and we snuck in the side door. I saw a few people looking at us a little funny. I was hoping we weren't going to get into trouble. I'm sure I was the first black athlete to work out at the club."

THROUGH THE MID TO late 1960s, the Auburn faithful were gradually realizing that an integrated sports program was coming, and some didn't like it. One irate fan wrote Jeff Beard, "It is beyond me why Auburn, in particular, or any other Southeastern Conference school, thinks they have to join the parade and go out and recruit Negro athletes. You will probably have enough trouble with that without going out and looking for it. It seems to me you should be concentrating on how to avoid the situation rather than plunging ahead to embrace it." The writer goes on to say that it is "just a simple fact of life that white men get along better with white men and Negroes with Negroes."[7]

Beard responded carefully, "I share many of your thoughts expressed in your letter, however, some that I do not. . . . At the present time we are one of the few schools in the Southeast that do not have colored athletes. However, we have had two or three visit our campus expressing desire to come to Auburn to be part of our athletic program. So far none have met the academic or athletic requirements. I do not know what the future holds for our athletic program."[8]

Beard's personal feelings about the coming desegregation of Auburn athletics were probably mixed. Every year, the issues and the stakes escalated. In 1966, the Texas Western University (now the University of Texas at El Paso) Miners beat the University of Kentucky Wildcats to win the NCAA basketball tournament. This basketball game was a significant cultural event, and sports historians agree that it helped usher in the desegregation of collegiate athletics. Texas Western was an integrated basketball team coached by Clem Haskins. The all-white University of Kentucky team was coached by the legendary Adolph Rupp, a segregationist who had coached Kentucky's basketball team for 42 years. The country watched as Haskins started five black players and used only two subs, both also black, to beat Kentucky 72 to 65. Many saw the game as a stark message that segregated Southern sports teams could no longer win if they continued to exclude talented African American athletes. Rupp was angry about the loss. Sportswriter Frank Fitzpatrick wrote, "Even as the jubilant Miners celebrated, a new set of myths was emerging. Rupp's lingering bitterness helped paint the Miners as urban street thugs, quasi-professionals imported from Northern cities to win Haskins a championship."[9]

After the historic game, Beard wrote Rupp congratulating him on Kentucky's otherwise superb season. "I would like to congratulate you and the Kentucky basketball team on the way that you have represented the Southeastern Conference during the season and in the NCAA Playoffs. . . . Those of us here at Auburn still feel that you have the best team and should be the national champions. I certainly feel that your team is the Caucasian national champions to say the least."[10] In hindsight, this comment makes it clear that Beard, who grew up in a segregated South, had conflicted feelings about the changes that were occurring. But although Beard never pushed for an integrated sports program at Auburn, he was caught in the wave of change and eventually would reluctantly give Rosen and other Auburn head coaches permission to recruit African American athletes.

Still, the change was slow. In the mid-1960s, when Alabama's white universities began scheduling games against schools in the North, school officials consistently refused to play against any team with African American players, even if the games were held in the North.[11] In November 1965, Eddie Sears, sports columnist for the *Miami Herald* and *St. Petersburg Times*, wrote to Jeff Beard with a set of questions regarding Auburn's willingness to play against any team in the SEC that fielded an integrated team: "As you may know a Negro basketball player is presently working out with the University of Florida team . . . there is the possibility he may play ball for the Gators. . . . Would Auburn play a team that had Negro athletes?"

Beard responded that Auburn would play any SEC team regardless of whether that team had African American players. "The questions you ask I don't feel are too important. If the University of Florida has a Negro on their basketball team, he will still be a member of the team and the University of

Florida is a member of the Southeastern Conference and Auburn University plays all members of the Southeastern Conference."[12]

By the end of the 1960s, some coaches in the SEC had begun playing teams with black athletes. Auburn University hosted its first home football game against an integrated foe, Wake Forest University, in September 1966. The following year, the University of Kentucky recruited Jim Green, its first African American football player (and track star, as mentioned in the previous chapter). The most famous integrated home game played by the University of Alabama occurred in 1970 when the University of Southern California squad, which included some 20 black players, handed Alabama an embarrassing 42–21 loss.

Rosen: "It was an exciting time because things were changing in the SEC. I was glad to see the changes, both from a personal and coaching point of view. When we saw how Green from Kentucky dominated the SEC Championship in the 100 and 220 it was another reminder that Auburn couldn't compete at the highest levels without African American runners."

Auburn's coaches were discussing among themselves when black athletes would play for Auburn. "By the mid-1960s the talk among the coaches was that we were going to have African American athletes participate on our teams and that Auburn would probably follow the lead of the University of Alabama. There was some differences of opinion about recruiting African Americans, some tense moments. Coach Nix [Auburn's head baseball coach] had reservations about playing black athletes. We figured the first African American athlete at Auburn would be on the football or basketball team."

In 1968 Bill Lynn, head basketball coach, became the first Auburn coach in any sport to offer an athletic scholarship to a black athlete. The offer went to Joby Wright, a high school star from Savannah, Georgia, but at the last minute Wright decided not to accept.

Lynn then turned his sights to the small west Alabama town of Boligee and offered a scholarship to Henry Harris. Thus, Harris became the first black athlete at Auburn when he accepted a basketball scholarship. Harris had a successful career at Auburn, was one of the most popular athletes on the team, and was named captain his final year. But Harris's important role in the desegregation of Auburn athletics was to be touched by tragedy. At 24 years of age and just two years after leaving Auburn, before earning his degree, Harris accepted an offer from Rudy Davalos to complete his degree as Davalos's assistant at the University of Wisconsin at Milwaukee. Davalos had previously been an assistant at Auburn, had coached Harris, and had a good rapport with him. It was a generous offer, but Davalos left soon after Harris arrived and his plan for his former player to graduate never materialized. Living so far from home proved difficult for Harris, and sometime during the raw winter months his life spiraled out of control. Far from his home, isolated from friends and family, Harris became severely depressed and committed suicide by jumping from his thirteenth-floor dorm room.

Harris is remembered for courageously opening the door to Auburn's sports programs for other African American athletes four years after Harold Franklin had integrated Auburn's academic programs. The desegregation of other sports at Auburn soon followed Harris's arrival. James Owens became Auburn's first black football player when he was awarded a scholarship in 1969. That began the progression of other black football players to enroll at Auburn: Cedric McIntyre, Mitzi Jackson, Jimmy Brock, Reese McCall, and Thom Gossom (the first walk-on to earn a scholarship). By 1972, seven of Auburn's 30 football scholarships were awarded to black athletes. In basketball, four of the five starters were black.

While there were growing pains during Auburn's progression towards racial diversity, the fact is that Auburn desegregated all of its sports programs with little or no disruption or protest.

Auburn was also slowly changing in other ways. In the 1950s and '60s, life in the South included a "rigid social order and a sense of place."[13] But by the 1970s that social order was breaking down. Civil rights, the Vietnam War, feminism, and the assassinations of John Kennedy, Robert Kennedy, and Martin Luther King Jr. were monumental events that triggered significant social and institutional shifts at universities across the country. While Auburn would never be confused with activist campuses like the University of California-Berkeley or the University of Wisconsin-Madison, Auburn also was becoming more diverse and more open, but at its own, deliberate pace.

Not only were there fewer than 200 black students attending Auburn in the early 1970s, but the university also had no tenure-track African American professors. Auburn hired historian Robert D. Reid as its first African American professor in 1972, and then only after pressure from the Afro-American Committee, a campus group that had sent a list of grievances to President Philpott. Among the demands was for Auburn to increase its black students and faculty. Reid, a native of Alabama, earned his doctorate in history from the University of Minnesota and began his teaching career at Tuskegee Institute (now University). He served on Auburn's history faculty for nine years before retiring. Reid faced barriers being the first African American professor at Auburn. For example, in 1972 he was encouraged by Professor Allen Jones, head of Auburn's history department, to join the Alabama Historical Association. Jones and others within the organization had been pushing it to admit blacks for some time. Reid was initially rejected because of his race, but when Jones and others protested the rejection, he subsequently became the first African American member of the AHA.[14]

THOUGH ROSEN WAS GIVEN permission to recruit black athletes in 1971, he was not successful until 1972. He feels the basketball and football teams led the way for other sports at Auburn in desegregation "because there was so much more pressure to win for football and basketball. Alabama was integrating their teams and Auburn didn't want to fall behind. If we didn't recruit black athletes, we couldn't complete successfully against schools who did."

Rosen understood that he couldn't compete in the Southeastern Conference without black athletes. For Rosen and other coaches, the decision to recruit black athletes wasn't an act of social justice or a political statement, but was a decision based on practicality. Black athletes would help Auburn teams to win.

In an interview with John Beck of the *Plainsman,* Rosen said, "We don't recruit someone because we know he's black but because we know he will be valuable to our program."[15] Rosen continued to play a limited role in Auburn's transition to the integration of its athletic teams. He never used his name or his position to publicly push for civil rights. "I never was out there about calling for integration. I wanted changes, but if I pushed the administration, I probably would have been fired. And what good would that have done?"

Finally given the green light to sign black athletes, "I recruited them hard and tried to make them successful on the track and in the classroom. This approach was the best one for me," Rosen said.

One obstacle Rosen, Lynn, and other coaches at Auburn faced was the perception among many black athletes that Auburn wasn't a supportive environment. Football player Thom Gossom said, "The problem is that a lot of black players in the state favor [the University of] Alabama where there is more social life."[16]

When he recruited Ray Crump, the 1971 Florida state high school champion in the 440-yard dash, Rosen had a frank discussion with him about Auburn's racial climate and whether the school would be a good fit. Crump told Rosen that he wasn't concerned about whether he could adapt to Auburn. "I went to an integrated high school my final two years. This experience helped prepare me to attend a school like Auburn. I remember Coach Rosen telling me that Auburn would be a friendly campus where I would be successful in track and in the classroom." Rosen's prediction turned out to be correct. "Auburn was a great place for me to go to school," Crump recalls. "I don't remember experiencing any racial problems while I was at school. I have good memories of my time at Auburn."

Clifford Outlin came along a few years later and said he doesn't recall any racial incidents during his time at Auburn, but that he nonetheless spent much of his free time away from the university. He was finding that while Auburn's classrooms were integrated, the campus was socially segregated. While Auburn had some 600 African American students attending classes by 1974, most felt left out of the campus social mainstream. That reality was very slow to change. As late as the mid-1980s, U.S. District Judge U. W. Clemon commented in an opinion in *Knight v. Alabama* (the long-running discrimination suit brought by the state's historically black universities seeking equity in education funding), "Black student participation in campus life at Auburn University is lower than that of any other public college."[17]

Outlin recalls, "I spent most of my [leisure] time in the black section of Auburn. There were no black fraternity houses on campus. There was more to do off campus." He also regularly traveled about 30 miles to Tuskegee Institute, the famous African American school of Booker T. Washington and George Washington Carver, to have a social life. "I just felt more comfortable in Tuskegee and was able to meet more people than I could have if I spent all my time on Auburn's campus."

Hurdler James Walker's first months at Auburn in the fall of 1975 were difficult. He liked the team and coaches, but he felt uncomfortable in some classes. "It was culture shock for me. My high school in Atlanta was all black. When I went to classes at Auburn all I saw was a sea of white faces. It took some time getting used to." By the end of the first semester he began to feel more at home. "Auburn turned out to be a great place for me. I was successful in the classroom and on the track. Coach Rosen played a great role in all my successes at Auburn. His sense of humor helped put things in perspective."

Rosen regrets he wasn't more proactive in making sure his athletes not only competed together but also socialized more together across racial lines. "I'm sure I could have done more, been more sensitive about the social structure of the team. Being a Jew, I've felt exclusion. But my main focus, and it always was, was to win track meets."

IN ADDITION TO RECRUITING African Americans, Rosen had another Auburn minority on his mind—his own—and in some ways recruiting Jewish students proved even more difficult.

Auburn in the early 1960s wasn't exactly a gathering place for Jewish students or athletes. Most of the Jewish students in Alabama elected to attend the University of Alabama because of its excellent Jewish studies program and its established Jewish fraternity. In Rosen's 28-year head coaching career at Auburn, he successfully recruited only three Jewish athletes. Auburn simply wasn't an attractive place for many Jewish students. "It wasn't until the 1980s that the A&P carried bagels in its frozen food section. What Jewish kid doesn't want a bagel in the morning? How can you attract Jewish athletes to a small Southern town? And just as importantly, there weren't Jewish girls."

One person who had complete confidence in Rosen was Rabbi Eugene

Blachschleger, his old friend from the mid-1950s. Blachschleger wrote to Rosen after he was promoted to head track coach: "A hearty congratulations to you and Joan on your promotion. I'm sure you will be a great success and continue to be a role model for Jewish athletes and fans everywhere."

Rosen did serve as a role model. He received an occasional letter from young athletes looking for Jewish sportsmen to admire. A boy from Maryland wrote for an autographed picture of Rosen to add to his collection of Jewish sports figures. Rosen: "There weren't many Jewish track and field athletes to choose from. I remember the old joke: 'What's the shortest book ever written?' The answer: 'Famous Jews in Sports.'"

Rosen recruited two promising Jewish athletes from Birmingham in the 1960s—the previously mentioned brothers Alvin and Milton Bresler. Alvin, the older, played end on the football team and ran hurdles for the track team from 1968 to 1971. Milton competed for Auburn track from 1970–72 and placed in the 440-yard hurdles in the SEC conference meet for three consecutive years. He also competed in the 1973 Maccabiah Games in Israel and won the intermediate hurdles. Rosen, who had a long-time interest in the Maccabiah Games, set up Bresler's trip to Jerusalem.

Vlad Soran, an Israeli from Tel Aviv, was the third Jewish athlete Rosen recruited. Rosen met Soran when he was coach in the 1985 Maccabiah Games and was impressed with his potential as a triple jumper. But Soran lasted only one year and left Auburn for the University of Maryland after the 1986–87 season. Rosen, in an interview with the *Buffalo Jewish Review*, explained it didn't work out for Soran because of Auburn's lack of "*Yiddishkeit*."

ROSEN WAS AWARE THAT social life and cultural comfort were not the only problems Auburn's minority athletes might face. As mentioned, baseball Coach Paul Nix never seemed comfortable with Rosen's Jewishness and both Nix and Athletic Director Jeff Beard struggled to overcome their segregationist upbringings and instincts. Some faculty members were also unwelcoming to black athletes.

Theo Abstom, a high school state champion middle distance runner from Mobile, competed for Auburn from 1977 to 1980. He won the 800 meters in both the 1979 and 1980 SEC championships. He remembers problems with a faculty member that still burn 30 years later.

During his sophomore year, he turned in an essay that he had spent considerable time writing. When the professor returned the papers, she asked Abstom to remain after class. "She told me she had read my paper and didn't believe I wrote my own paper. She said there was no way I was a good writer. She told me I had to write another paper with her watching me. I tried to tell her I wrote the paper and I had another class right after her class that I didn't want to miss." She required Abstom to stay after class and write for the hour in her presence. What Abston remembers mostly about that incident was that "she never apologized to me after she saw I could write. I didn't like that, but most of all I didn't like missing class that day."

For the most part, however, Abstom feels that "Auburn was a great place to go to school. We were a close-knit team." He credits Rosen's honesty and sense of humor for making the team a cohesive unit.

Frank Litsky, *New York Times* sports columnist for more than 50 years, saw firsthand how Rosen was able to communicate with white and black athletes: "Mel didn't have a hidden agenda. Athletes respond to that type of honesty." Thom Gossom recalls, "Mel was one of the good ones at Auburn. The black athletes felt they could talk to him. We trusted him. Mel was a city guy and knew how to relate to us."

7

The Fabulous Five

(1973–81)

"What was our recruiting strategy? It was simple, Clifford Outlin brought in Willie Smith, Willie brought in Harvey Glance, and Harvey brought in everybody else."

Rosen considers his 1972 recruiting class the beginning of a new era for Auburn track because he successfully recruited an African American athlete. Typically, it didn't happen easily.

Jerry Smith, assistant coach 1971–77, played a central role in bringing in many high-profile athletes. Former Auburn Assistant Athletic Director Buddy Davidson saw firsthand Smith's significant role in recruiting many of Auburn's top track athletes in the early to mid 1970s. Smith brought to recruiting the same intensity and desire to be successful that had made him a track star at Auburn in the 1960s. When he hired Smith, Rosen told him to "kiss your wife goodbye and hit the road."

Smith didn't have to travel far to get verbal commitments from two black athletes in 1972: Harold Reese, who ran a 9.8 100-yard dash and cleared 6' 10" in the high jump, was from Auburn High School, and Johnny Williams, a sprinter who had the fastest 100-yard dash (9.5 seconds) in the country that year, hailed from nearby Talladega. But after verbally committing, neither enrolled. Reese decided at the last minute to join the Army, and Williams, who had academic problems in high school, wasn't able to get into Auburn despite Rosen's best efforts lobbying the admissions office. Losing both athletes was a blow to the program. Smith learned an important lesson about recruiting wars in the SEC. "This taught me to never let up with recruiting even after an athlete commits. You've got to keep the pressure on. I said to myself this won't happen to me again."

Rosen had another African American athlete in his sights, Ray Crump, a sprinter and middle-distance runner from Tallahassee, Florida. Crump was the state high school champion in the 440-yard dash. Rosen had been watching Crump's high school performance for two years. Florida State University was also interested. Rosen's only concern about Crump was that he had sustained several leg injuries that sidelined him for much of his senior year. There was a risk that Crump might not hold up to the rigors of a lengthy collegiate track schedule. But Rosen was confident that by under-training, using frequent but shorter, less intensive workouts, Crump could be a healthy, productive runner for Auburn. Rosen was sure his Alabama Hall of Fame trainer, Kenny Howard, could keep Crump on the track.

He traveled to Tallahassee and met with Crump and his mother at their home. Crump remembers Rosen's recruiting visit. "I was excited about the possibility of attending Auburn. I wanted to get out of Tallahassee. But I didn't know what my mother would say about me going away to school. She wanted me to stay at home."

At the beginning of Rosen's recruiting visit, there was some tension between Rosen and Crump's mother. "My mother didn't want me to get taken advantage of. She was worried Coach Rosen was only interested in track and nothing else." She began questioning Rosen about the likelihood Ray would earn a degree if he came to Auburn. "Coach Rosen was sitting on our couch and my mother kept insisting he guarantee that I would earn my degree. She wasn't going to let me go to Auburn without making Coach Rosen answer a few questions."

Rosen also remembers Crump's mother and their discussion. "She was not too different from my mother. She was protective of her son. I told Mrs. Crump that I couldn't guarantee a degree, but I promised her that I would do everything in my power to make sure Ray went to class and had every opportunity to graduate. She had a great relationship with Raymond. I understood that she didn't want us to exploit Ray and not look out for his academic interests."

When Rosen went to Crump's high school to examine his academic record he found that his potential recruit's class standing was too low to be admitted to Auburn. Rosen's philosophy was always to give an athlete an opportunity even if his high school academic record was below Auburn's standards. "Over the years I've seen kids with good grades and high SAT scores do poorly in school and I have seen athletes with poor grades and low SAT scores thrive. The bottom line is—some college is better than none at all."

Rosen next visited Crump's school counselor. He asked if she could help Crump get into Auburn. "The lady was not interested in helping in any way. She said that she didn't think Ray was college material, particularly for a school like Auburn. She predicted that he would flunk out. I was shocked at the racism and her unwillingness to give Ray the benefit of the doubt. We talked a long time, and I asked her to help me give Ray a chance. Over the course of our conversation she warmed up to the idea of helping him. I suggested that we could include all the dropouts from that year and recalculate his class standing. She agreed and with the adjustment of rankings he made the cut-off and could enter Auburn."

Crump's mother finally relented and gave permission for him to attend Auburn, making him the first African American athlete to attend Auburn on a track scholarship. Crump was well worth the effort; he ran on the 400-meter relay team that placed in the conference championships three times, and he earned All American status in 1976. He was named team captain his senior year. Most importantly, Crump not only graduated in four years but went on to have a distinguished career in the Army.

Also in 1972, Rosen recruited Bret Dull, a discus thrower and shot putter from Winter Park, Florida. Dull was an "A" student and had excelled in the prestigious Golden West Invitational Track Meet in California his senior year. He ranked as one of the best high school discus throwers in the country. Rosen was most impressed with Dull's enormous potential. He was a lanky 6'8" and 220 pounds. And for a big man, he was a graceful athlete. Rosen felt that if Dull worked hard in the weight room he had the potential to be one of the best collegiate discus throwers in the NCAA. Rosen's predictions were accurate. Dull was an immediate success. He won the discus in the 1973 SEC conference meet and qualified for the NCAA championships along with teammates Jim Carson, a high hurdler, and Tim Curry, a 440-yard hurdler.

In the course of Dull's freshman year, Rosen learned that his star athlete was a free spirit. After the conference championships Rosen was informed that Dull had been stopped by campus security for streaking nude across campus. When Rosen met with Dull to find out what happened, Dull informed him that he and some friends were bored and they decided to streak that night (streaking was then the rage across college campuses). "I couldn't believe it. When I asked him if he had thought about getting caught he said he didn't think anyone would recognize him. I looked up at him and asked if he was out of his mind—how many 6'8" naked guys are on campus!" Rosen ended the meeting by telling Dull to keep his clothes on.

Dull's second track season was not quite as successful even though he placed second in the discus in the 1974 conference championships. Rosen was troubled by Dull's poor work ethic in the weight room; he was spending less and less time with his teammates working out. And when he did show up for his workouts, Rosen felt he wasn't working hard enough. Rosen talked to Dull about his concerns several times during the 1974 season. But Dull was resistant to commit to an intensive weight-training program. While Rosen was never sure why Dull didn't like lifting weights, some of his teammates had their opinions about the dispute between Rosen and their teammate. Crump, a team leader, felt that Dull "wasn't the most motivated athlete" and just didn't "want to extend the effort."

In the spring of 1974, the difference of opinion between Rosen and Dull came to a head because Dull was badmouthing the track program to Rob Will, a freshman shot putter and discus thrower. Dull tried to discourage him from following the designated workouts. Dull's negative campaign crossed the line with Rosen. What most aggravated Rosen was that Will, at six feet and 200 pounds, was an undersized shot putter, and needed to get bigger and stronger to compete successfully. Rosen worried that Dull would be a negative influence on the freshman's development. What Rosen didn't know at the time was that Will was an avid weight lifter and one of the hardest-working athletes on the team and would not be influenced by Dull.

Rosen finally dismissed Dull from the team. "There was no arguing, no hard feelings, but I couldn't let him stay on the team. He was a disruptive influence, particularly for the younger athletes. We were better off as a team without him. It was a shame because Bret was an excellent student and had great potential as an athlete."

Rosen spent considerable time trying to increase Will's size and strength. The results came slowly, but after two years of training, Will got bigger and stronger. The extra muscle made a difference; he placed third in the 1978 conference championships and second in the conference in 1979. That same year Will placed fourth in the NCAA. Rosen was particularly pleased with Will's success. He didn't have the greatest natural ability, but by following workouts he became a consistent performer for Auburn. Will's transformation didn't go unnoticed by other coaches. After Will's second-place finish at the conference championships a coach from another team came up to Rosen and said, "When did you guys start using steroids?" The use of performance-enhancing drugs was becoming a major concern in SEC track and field. "I couldn't believe it. Here was a guy who worked his rear end off and got bigger and stronger through hard work and someone accuses him of using steroids. Even then drugs were killing our sport."

COLLEGIATE RECRUITING IS THE lifeblood of an athletic program's success. It was because of Rosen's and Smith's recruiting efforts that the track program improved from a last-place finish in the SEC in 1972 to a fourth-place finish in 1974. This success helped Rosen gain stature within the athletic department. While relationships among coaches of the different sports were generally positive, coaches who didn't win were often the target of barbs from some of the others. Claude Saia was an assistant football coach in the early 1970s. Winning was everything to the gregarious Saia. Not only did he want to see Auburn win football games, but he took pride if other teams at Auburn also won. Saia would invariably ask each Monday morning during track season, "Rosen, how did your guys do this weekend?" Auburn track was struggling at the time and was competing in mostly dual meets. Most of the time, Rosen had to tell Saia that they had lost. When Saia heard about Auburn's poor finish several weeks in a row he told Rosen, "You guys better put it in gear and win some meets. You've got to get out there and recruit the guys who can win." This scenario played out much of the season, with Saia's comments to Rosen becoming more and more biting. Finally, after tiring of Saia's predictable barbs, Rosen replied to Saia's standard question, "Rosen how did you guys do this weekend?" with, "We came in second." Saia looked at Rosen, thought for a moment and said, "Great work! You guys are finally improving. Keep it up!"

Rosen recalled, "He didn't realize our second place was in a dual meet."

A major factor in Auburn's surprising fourth place finish in the 1974 conference meet was the performance of Clifford Outlin, who won the 100-yard dash and anchored the 400-meter relay team. Outlin, from Birmingham, spent two years at Calhoun Junior College on a basketball scholarship before attending Auburn. Outlin's dream was to play basketball for the University of Alabama. But at 5'8", he was talented but judged too short to compete at the Division I level, and Alabama didn't offer Outlin a scholarship. He thought it was Alabama's loss: "I was small but few could outjump me and nobody could outrun me on the court."

Despite his love of basketball, Outlin's best sport was track. He was the state high school champion in the 100-yard dash in 1973. Rosen sent Jerry Smith to visit Outlin. Smith made his case to Outlin's mother why Auburn was the best school for her son. Mrs. Outlin took a liking to Smith and eventually steered Clifford to accept a full scholarship in track from Auburn. Outlin: "I always did what my mother told me to do, so I signed with Auburn. But my love of basketball never left me. During my years at Auburn, I stayed in shape by playing basketball with some of the varsity basketball players. In fact, they encouraged me to go out for the team. I don't know if Coach Rosen knew that. He wouldn't have liked it."

Rosen credits Outlin with turning the track program around. "By signing Outlin we got the high-profile sprinter we needed to bring in other great sprinters. The top athletes want to go to a program with other great athletes. He was the first of our great sprinters. We wanted Auburn to be known as the place for the best sprinters."

Outlin immediately became a leader and was elected captain by his teammates. "I think I was one of the first black team captains at Auburn. I was proud of that, still am." He has high regard for Rosen. "I loved Coach.

You could talk to him. He was an important reason why I was successful at Auburn. Coach knew how to train you so you wouldn't get injuries. He had a great sense of humor."

At Auburn, Outlin developed into a world-class sprinter, running the world's fastest 60-meter dash in 6.4 in 1975. He was on target to earn a spot on the 1976 Olympics in Montreal. However, just before Outlin was to travel to Eugene, Oregon, to qualify for the Olympic team, he turned pro. The Professional Track League had just formed and representatives from the league invited him to compete. Rosen tried to talk him out of it, arguing that participating in the 1976 Olympic Games would be an experience he would never forget. And a gold medal might be more lucrative in the long run than running pro track. Rosen was skeptical that the PTL could last, but Outlin decided to run for the money. "I needed money fast to help my family and going pro seemed like the best choice at the time." Outlin won his first race and collected $600 for his effort. The win fueled Outlin's optimism about his prospects for big earnings on the pro track circuit. Unfortunately, just as Rosen predicted, the league folded shortly thereafter and Outlin missed his chance to compete in the Montreal Olympics. "I have regretted that decision for a long time," he says. Rosen adds, "I felt bad for Clifford. He made a bad decision. I just couldn't talk him out of it."

UNIONDALE HIGH SCHOOL ON Long Island, New York, was a rich source of athletes for Rosen in the 1970s and 1980s. Uniondale's head track coach, Al Krauser, was a close friend. Both had grown up in Brooklyn and both were Jews. Krauser even knew several of Rosen's friends from his Lincoln High School days. Krauser would eventually serve on Rosen's staff when he was head coach of the American team at the Maccabiah Games in Israel.

Rosen's connection to Krauser proved helpful as Willie Smith, known as "the Long Island Express" and rated the number one high school sprinter in the United States in 1974, ran for Uniondale High School. Krauser had been lobbying Smith to attend Auburn. While it was a long shot that a black kid from New York would want to attend a Southern school like Auburn, the charismatic Clifford Outlin was a big drawing card for Smith. He had met Outlin and was impressed with his accomplishments. Jerry Smith and

Rosen made several recruiting visits to Uniondale in 1974, and Krauser assured his star runner that he would adjust easily to Auburn track and the climate in the South was conducive for training. Rosen's quiet demeanor also helped to convince Smith that Auburn was his best choice. Krauser remembers talking to Smith and telling him why he should go to Auburn. "Willie liked coaches who were quiet, not yellers. I told Willie running for Mel would be like running for me." After several recruiting visits Willie Smith verbally committed to Auburn. Rosen thought Smith had the potential to be a national champion sprinter. In an interview with the *Plainsman*, Smith expressed his reasons for selecting Auburn. "I could have gone to just about any school, but it seemed that athletes and students are treated well at Auburn. There is just a friendly atmosphere here."[1]

Just before signing day, however, Auburn almost lost its prized recruit. Krauser tipped off Jerry Smith that a coach from another university was scheduled to visit Willie Smith on signing day and had a good chance of changing the young athlete's mind about attending Auburn. Jerry Smith took immediate action to keep his number one recruit. "I called several friends around the country and told them to call Willie at his school at 15-minute intervals the entire morning. When he began talking to the recruiter, Willie was constantly paged to come to the office to take a telephone call." After a couple of hours of having Smith constantly leaving the room to take phone calls, the recruiter from the University of Florida gave up. "Who needs the aggravation," the angry coach complained to Krauser as he stormed out.

Willie Smith had a spectacular career at Auburn. He won three NCAA championships, won the 440-yard dash in 1977 and 1978, and was named All American three consecutive years. Smith was fiercely competitive and at times extremely emotional. One of Smith's favorite meets, a meet he waited for each year, was Auburn's dual meet against Alabama. In 1978 Auburn was in Tuscaloosa running against Alabama. The meet, as usual, was close. Smith was in the best shape of his career when he took his place at the starting line for the 400-meter dash. Smith told Rosen right before the race that he was going to do something special; he said he just felt it. The conditions were perfect for Smith to run his best. At the gun, Smith exploded out of the blocks and ran away from the competition. As Smith crossed the finish line, Rosen knew Smith had indeed done something special—his 44.73 was the fastest in the world. Smith became so excited after he heard the announcement he hyperventilated and collapsed. He had to be carried off the track.

Rosen recalls, "Smith couldn't run the 4x400-meter relay. He was totally out of commission. We ended up losing the race and losing the meet. I remember Willie being carried off and him waving to me saying, 'Good luck, Coach.' It was the first and last time an athlete's world-best performance cost me a meet."

Smith was one of the few athletes to qualify for three Olympic teams in track and field: 1976 in Montreal, 1980 in Moscow, and 1984 in Los Angeles.

Smith had come to Auburn as a sprinter but switched to the 400 for the 1976 season after Harvey Glance was recruited. Smith couldn't beat Glance in the 100 or 200. This really bothered Smith. Rosen remembers how Smith reacted: "Willie asked to run the 400. He was not too happy losing to Harvey all the time. Willie used to say to everyone that I made him into a 400 man. I said, 'No, Willie, Harvey made you into a 400 man.'"

THE 1975 RECRUITING CLASS featured three highly touted athletes: Harvey Glance, James Walker, and Tony Easley. They, along with veterans Willie Smith and John Lewter, became known in the press as the "Fabulous Five" and were instrumental in Auburn capturing four straight SEC indoor championships, 1976 through 1979. The "Fabulous Five" was recognized by *Track and Field News* as the most dominant group of athletes in American track in the 1970s.

Harvey Glance was one of six high school sprinters to run a 9.5 second 100-yard dash in his senior year. Glance, from Phenix City, Alabama, lived just 20 miles from Auburn. Rosen and Jerry Smith spent significant time visiting Glance at his home. But they had stiff competition from the University of Southern California and Southern Illinois University for Glance's considerable talents. Not only was Glance an accomplished sprinter, he had long-jumped over 24 feet. Rosen had seen Glance compete in several meets and was more impressed each time. "He was a natural sprinter. His running form was excellent. I was most impressed with his work ethic.

He was highly motivated and was dreaming about going to the Olympics even in high school." In his senior year English class, Glance wrote a paper outlining his Olympic aspirations and detailing how he was going to win a gold medal. His insensitive teacher tore up the paper in front of him saying, "Don't write nonsense." The incident only inspired Glance. "It ate at me, wanting to fulfill that dream."[2]

The NCAA had not yet limited the number of visits a college coach could make to a recruit, and Rosen spent many evenings in Glance's home watching television with the young athlete. "Harvey was shy. He wasn't a big talker. So most of the time Harvey, his sister, and I sat in the dark and watched *Sanford and Son*. I can tell you the plot of most of the episodes."

Glance did choose Auburn, not just because of Rosen and Smith's bi-weekly visits, but because he wanted to stay close to home. "Harvey was a mama's boy," says James Walker, one of Glance's best friends on the team. Glance wanted to attend school close to his mom. "She was sick at the time," Glance recalls, "so I didn't want to go to school halfway across the country. I also was impressed with Coach Rosen. He was a great coach, the very best." But Glance says it was "the atmosphere" at Auburn that ultimately swayed him. "When I was being recruited, I visited schools all over the country and no one reached out and touched me like Auburn did."

Rosen saw something more in Glance than just his running ability. Rosen remembers first seeing Glance on the track. "I could tell immediately by talking to him and watching him train that he was the most dedicated athlete I ever saw. When Harvey came to Auburn, I knew we had something special. A great competitor."

New York Times columnist Frank Litsky saw Rosen develop an almost paternal relationship with Glance. "Harvey was Mel's kind of athlete. He loved Harvey's dedication to the sport. With Mel and Harvey, track came first. They were similar that way. They were kindred spirits." Glance would often refer to his coach as "Daddy." Litsky remembers Rosen saying that "Harvey is the son I never had." Their relationship continued long after Glance stopped competing as an athlete.

Glance, like most high-profile athletes, learned quickly that once enrolled, the lavish attention and promises made during the recruiting period sometimes evaporate. Glance became homesick after about two weeks on campus and decided to go home for the weekend. Because he had no transportation, he went to Rosen and asked him if he would drive him to visit his parents. "I told Harvey that it was against NCAA rules for me to drive him home. I told him his best bet was to get out to the highway and stick out his thumb." Glance had remembered Rosen telling him that if he attended Auburn he could visit his parents anytime he wanted. "I didn't realize hitchhiking would be part of my travel plans."

JAMES WALKER WAS A high-profile high school hurdler from Atlanta. Jerry Smith made several visits to Walker's home to convince the young man to attend Auburn on a scholarship. It was a difficult proposition. Before Smith's visit, Walker had not considered Auburn and wasn't familiar with any aspect of Auburn's track program. He was also not keen on living in a small town in Alabama. After several visits, however, Smith convinced Walker to sign a letter of intent. Because Smith spent considerable time recruiting Walker, the young man assumed he was the head coach. When Walker first stepped onto Auburn's track he learned otherwise. "I remember getting warmed up and this guy comes up to me and starts telling me what workout I should do. I looked up at him and asked 'who are you?' It was Coach Rosen. That was our first meeting. I'll never forget it. I thought, who is this guy. Little did I know at the time what a profound impact he would have on my life."

Tony Easley, from Roanoke, Virginia, was a lesser known recruit but had run a 9.8 hundred in his senior year. Rosen saw Easley's potential. "Tony improved more than any athlete I ever coached. By Tony's senior year he was running a 9.4 hundred, a significant improvement from his freshman year."

When these athletes arrived on campus, they didn't waste any time showing their dominance on the track. In their first intrasquad meet Glance broke the school record in the 100, and Walker broke the record in the intermediate hurdles. The veterans on the team took notice of their new teammates. Rosen: "I'll never forget that intrasquad meet. I knew by adding Harvey, James, and Tony we were going to be a force in the conference and nationally. It was a good day!"

THE U.S. TRIALS FOR the 1976 Montreal Olympics were held June 19–27 in Eugene, Oregon. Two runners from Auburn qualified for the team; Harvey Glance in the 100 and the 400-meter relay, and Willie Smith as an alternate on the 400-meter relay. Glance won the 100 in spectacular fashion. Houston McTear, the Baker (Florida) High School phenomenon who had run a 9.0 in the 100-yard dash, got the best start and led at 50 meters, when he was caught by the surging Glance who won with a time of 10.11. In the 100-meter finals Willie Smith was in third place at the 80-meter mark but was edged out by Steve Riddick at the finish line. "Willie ran a hard 100 but there were faster runners that day. Willie was excitable and didn't run as relaxed as he could have and it cost him." Smith just missed qualifying for the 400, but he earned a spot as one of the alternates on the 4x100 relay team.

Rosen took his entire family to Montreal. He thought the Montreal Games would be historic. "The trend had been for the last several competitions, the country hosting the Olympics lost a lot of money. I thought that after Montreal no other country would want to host the event. I wanted my kids to see what I thought would be the last Olympics. I'm glad I was wrong."

Both Glance and Smith were running their best at the beginning of the Olympic competition. Rosen had given them workouts to use in the days leading to their races. Both were confident about their chances to bring home gold.

Hasely Crawford from Eastern Michigan University, Don Quarry from Jamaica, and the great Russian sprinter Valeriy Borzov were Harvey Glance's main competition in the 100 meters. Glance was running the best of his career. He hadn't lost in the 100-meters the entire season. Glance, like always, was supremely confident he would win the event. Rosen watched the 100-meter finals from the stands. He studied Glance as he warmed up and felt Glance looked relaxed, ready to go. "I thought Harvey had a great chance to win. But he needed to get out of the blocks fast and run relaxed. The key for Harvey was the start. But the officials delayed the start of the race, and I worried Harvey might be affected by that. You have to remember Harvey was only 19." Glance describes what happened during the delay. "We were set up in the blocks and someone says we need to come in because they had to get the woman's javelin ceremonies ready. So they put us in a room and I started to think, think, think." Then he saw O. J. Simpson, who was a commentator for ABC. As the cameras trained on him, Glance heard Simpson say, "There is the favorite." It was then Glance remembers, "that the pressure erupted."

At the gun, Glance hesitated just slightly before exploding out of the blocks. His hesitation was costly as he was in fourth place after the first 50 meters. But Glance closed the distance quickly and was gaining on Borzov for third place. But with 10 meters to go he tired, tightened up, lost his form, and finished fourth behind winner Hasely Crawford. Glance took the loss hard. "Harvey didn't run his best race. When he got behind he tried to catch up too quickly and when he got tired his form fell apart. I was proud of how Harvey really closed the gap. He just panicked when he started poorly and never recovered."

Rosen left the stands quickly and found Glance sitting by himself in the athletic dorm, disconsolate over the lost opportunity to win a medal. "I talked to Harvey for three hours trying to boost him up. He felt he let everyone down by not winning. It was a tough three hours. Harvey was really upset. I kept telling him to forget the race and get prepared for the 400-meter relay." Glance did recover and helped the American team of Jonny Jones, Millard Hampton, and Steve Riddick win gold in the 400-meter relay.

When Glance returned home to his home in Phenix City he was given a hero's welcome. But Rosen found that some fans, rather than talking about Glance's gold medal in the relay and his impressive fourth place in the 100, asked why he didn't win the gold in the 100. They wanted to know what happened. "I was shocked. Rather than seeing what an incredible job he had done, they focused only on not getting a gold medal in the 100. They didn't understand being the fourth fastest person in the world was an incredible accomplishment."

Glance expressed his own disappointment at not winning the 100 in Montreal to the *Columbus Enquirer*: "The Olympics are supposed to be for individuals, but for a person like me, you think about your country. Not letting it down. I even thought about the people back in Phenix City, not letting them down."[3]

Over the years that followed, Rosen and Glance were often invited to give talks about their Olympic experiences. They continued to develop a close friendship during these times traveling across Alabama to different speaking engagements. On the way to one such engagement in Birmingham, they drove by a Ku Klux Klan parade in downtown Birmingham. Rosen and Glance, sitting side by side, watched as they waited for the procession to pass. They looked at each other, but neither said a word. They sat in silence for several minutes as the demonstrators moved on. "I remember there was a sadness in Harvey's eyes. I thought about saying something to him, but he knew how I felt and I knew how he felt." It was on one of these trips that Glance gave Rosen his Olympic watch as a token of appreciation for all his coach had done for him.

AUBURN HAD THE NUMBER one ranked 400-meter relay team in the country in 1977. Their time of 39.24 set the standard for all others. Rosen had a star-filled lineup. Tony Easley ran the first leg. He was "explosive out of the blocks, one of the best starters in the country." He handed off to John Lewter who "knew how to run the straightaway and was one of the most sure-handed relay men I ever coached. It was quite a sight to see such a big man with so much speed." Willie Smith ran third. "He was the second-fastest on the relay team and extended our lead most races. He ran the curve as well as anyone in the country. You know you have a good relay team when Willie Smith was only the second-fastest on the team." Auburn's anchor was Harvey Glance. "He was one of the fastest runners in the world who was able to time the baton exchange so he was running at top speed almost immediately. Nobody could catch Harvey. He knew how to close a race. He had the confidence required of an anchor. Harvey never considered the idea someone could beat him. He withstood pressure."

Frank Litsky tells how the relays change the character of track: "What was once an individual sport translates itself into a team effort."

A week or so before the 1977 NCAA championships, Rosen was contacted by an assistant coach with the Dallas Cowboys. He was interested in signing John Lewter to a football contract. While Lewter didn't play football at Auburn, he had played two years in high school. He looked like a football player; he was 6'3" and weighed over 200 pounds. Because of his blazing speed, Dallas considered him to be a great split-end prospect. Rosen told the coach they had one more meet, the nationals, and asked him to keep away from Lewter until after the season so as not to jeopardize his eligibility. Rosen then went to Lewter and told him about the Cowboys' interest. "I told Lewter to stay away from Dallas as it would cost him his eligibility if he signed a contract. I told him to wait until after the NCAA meet. The money would still be there."

Just days before Auburn was to travel to Champaign, Illinois, for the nationals, Rosen went to the bank. As soon as he walked in one of the tellers, who knew Rosen was the track coach, rushed up to him and asked if John Lewter was on his track team. She then told him Lewter had come in earlier to deposit a check from the Dallas Cowboys. A $50,000 check from the Dallas Cowboys was quite an event in the small-town bank. Rosen immediately knew the ramifications for Lewter and his relay team. "I found Lewter and told him he was ineligible for the NCAA meet. I asked him why he just didn't wait until the season was over before signing. He said he was excited about playing for Dallas and didn't want to miss the opportunity. I couldn't believe it. I called Gil Brandt, general manager of the Cowboys. I was hot. He said one of his new assistants must have contacted Lewter and sent him the check. Brandt said he had nothing to do with it. There was nothing I could do about it. Lewter was out. Without him our relay team placed fifth in the nationals. It was a real disappointment. We would have won if Lewter had run."

As it turned out nothing came of Lewter's football opportunity with Dallas. Lewter remembers the tough practices during his stay at Dallas before being cut. "Mike Ditka was our offensive line coach. He screamed, yelled and cursed a lot. Not like Coach Rosen. Ditka didn't make practice easy." To this day Lewter feels the Dallas staff never seriously looked at him. He felt he never got a fair chance to make the team. It was a bitter disappointment. "I regret how it turned out. I wish I had kept that check for a few more days before cashing it. We had the best relay team in the country, and I wish now that I would have run with them in the NCAAs."

ROSEN BUILT STRONG RELATIONSHIPS among his athletes through team discipline. His athletes generally liked each other, a rare occurrence in high-level collegiate sports. Harvey Glance remembers how Rosen never played favorites. "Because Mel treated everyone the same there was no jealousy on the team. It fostered team chemistry." Stars like Glance and James Walker were held to the same standard of behavior as others on the team. Rosen was a stickler for his athletes to arrive on time for practice. It was something he had learned from his Lincoln High School coach, Hy Schecter. One afternoon in 1977 Glance and Walker came to practice about 15 minutes late. They had been at the barber getting their hair braided and their appointment took longer than expected. When they finally arrived, both went to Rosen to explain why they were late. But before either could say a word, Rosen told them to go home. Glance remembers his anger as he left practice. "It was the one time I was mad, really mad at Coach Rosen. I felt he was being unfair because he wouldn't listen to our reason for being late. I went to my room and thought about transferring. James [Walker] was with me, and he talked to me and told me to settle down."

It took Glance some time before he understood why his coach wouldn't allow athletes to practice if they came late. "I finally realized Coach was right. He didn't play favorites. It helped with team discipline and helped us be a team, not just individual performers." In later years, Glance, as head track coach at Auburn and then the University of Alabama, would tell that story to his athletes. "I tell them that rules apply to everyone. I learned from Coach Rosen that you have to treat everyone the same if you are going to have discipline on the team. The message is be accountable for your behavior."

James Walker remembers how the team socialized as a group. "We did things together. Even as we were walking on the street we would pretend to be running in a race and passing the baton. We were a dedicated team. Harvey was important in keeping us united as a team. In spite of the intense competition, we were able to keep it in perspective." Lewter remembers that "we called each other partner, we were that close as a group." Tony Easley exemplified this commitment to the team. He spent much of his career at Auburn getting beaten by Harvey Glance in the 100. But placing second behind Glance for four years never dampened his enthusiasm about competing. "When Easley lost a race to Harvey, and it happened every meet they competed, Tony would come to me and say, 'Coach, I will get him next time.' This camaraderie was important in developing a dominant track team."

Easley's patience and dedication paid off. Glance was injured while preparing for the 1978 NCAA indoor championships, opening the door for Easley to emerge from his shadow. Easley placed fourth in the 60-yard dash and earned the recognition that had eluded him for so long. However, Auburn paid a price for Glance's absence. Auburn placed second, just behind the University of Texas at El Paso. "We would have been national champions had Harvey competed for us. He would have scored enough points in the sprints and the long jump to put us over the top. But it was nice to see Tony finally get his recognition and not have to hear, 'I'll get him next time, Coach.'"

Dave Pincus contacted Rosen in late 1976 about coaching the American track and field team at the 1977 Maccabiah Games. The Maccabiah Games, sometimes referred to as the Jewish Olympics, features Jewish athletes from countries around the world competing in all sports. The Games are held every four years in Ramat Gan near Tel Aviv. Pincus, the American representative for the Games, had the responsibility to select a coach for the track and field team. Pincus, a former track star at Penn State, had followed the success Rosen was having at Auburn and wanted him to coach the American team. "There was a small, but talented group of Jewish track and field coaches in the United States. Mel was the very best."

Rosen, like most Jews who were interested in athletics, was quite familiar with the Maccabiah Games. Rosen was a friend of Irv Mondschein, track coach at Penn State and head coach of the American team in the 1973 Maccabiah Games. Mondschein's stories about life in Israel intrigued Rosen. While Rosen was not a religious Jew, he was interested in most secular Jewish topics. Pincus called Rosen to ask if he would coach the U.S. team in Tel Aviv in 1977. "I said yes immediately. It was an honor to go to Israel and coach. I was appointed head track and field coach four times. It was on our first trip when I visited Yad Vashem [the National Holocaust Museum] that the full weight of the Holocaust hit me. I was proud to be a Jew. I understood the purpose of the Maccabiah Games was to give Jews from the United States and other countries an opportunity to learn about their Jewish heritage."

The hardest aspect of coaching in the Maccabiah Games was finding enough Jewish athletes to participate. Rosen jokes about the difficulty he had finding Jewish athletes. "At first we had to have a certificate from a rabbi stating that the athlete was Jewish for him or her to complete. Then the rules loosened up, and an athlete was eligible if he or she could show that either their mother or father was Jewish. No certification needed. But I still had trouble recruiting. There weren't that many around. It got to the point where I would have been willing to use anyone, regardless of their religion, as long as they were willing to just talk to a Jew!"

After recruiting athletes from around the country, Rosen finally selected 30 to join the team. Among the group was Milton Bresler, who had run for Rosen in the early 1970s.

In his first trip to Israel, Rosen was surprised to find the Israeli track and field team relatively weak. In subsequent years, however, the Israeli team improved dramatically. "When I went back to Israel, in 1981 they had a better team. The Israelis were recruiting Russian Jews to come and live in Israel and complete on their sports teams. The influx of the Russian Jews to Israel made them much stronger as a team." After his third coaching assignment in the Maccabiah Games in 1981, Rosen was asked if he was interested in staying in Israel and coach track and field. "I told them that I appreciated their interest in me, but I was happy coaching at Auburn."

IN 1977 ROSEN WAS named manager of the U.S. team at the World University Games in Sofia, Bulgaria. Harvey Glance, James Walker, and Willie Smith were named to the team. It was a difficult trip for everyone. While the track facilities were reasonably good, the living conditions and the food left something to be desired. Despite the conditions, the competition was fierce as the meet served as a prelude to the 1980 Olympics. In the 400 intermediate hurdles James Walker was disqualified for going over the outside of one of the hurdles. Rosen contested the disqualification but was overruled after a heated discussion. To this day, Walker doesn't believe he fouled. "I got out of the blocks fast and took a big lead. It was one of my best starts ever. I won the race by a wide margin, but then I was told I was disqualified. I was angry at the time. But there was nothing I could do about it. Coach Rosen protested my disqualification. I still don't believe my leg went outside the hurdle." Willie Smith fared better: he placed second in the 400. Harvey Glance was sixth in the 100 and anchored the sixth-place 400-meter relay.

As manager of the team, Rosen handled all aspects of the trip. He scheduled meetings, coordinated room assignments and meals, as well as posting the starting times for the races. Because of his role Rosen became the coach to go to with complaints about the conditions in Sofia. "The accommodations were not the best, and the meals were worse. I heard about it from some of the athletes. They weren't happy."

What Rosen most remembers, however, is one evening when everyone else was out experiencing the nightlife. Harvey Glance wanted to get in a weight-lifting workout, and he asked Rosen to help him find a gym. "We went looking and after an hour or so we finally found a gym. The only persons in the gym were two women—both Bulgarian shot putters. They weighed at least 275 pounds each, strong girls. So in walks Harvey, all of 140 pounds. He out-lifted both of them. The women couldn't believe how strong Harvey was. Everyone else is out on the town, and Harvey is getting in a workout. This tells you something important about Harvey. He was the most focused athlete I have ever coached."

AFTER ROSEN HAD GUIDED Auburn to four straight indoor SEC championships (1977–80) and an outdoor championship in 1979, he was named Southeastern Conference Coach of the Year. Rosen considers his 1979 team his best ever. That team scored points in 18 of the 20 events in the outdoor conference championships, winning seven first-place finishes. Harvey Glance won the 100 and the long jump. James Walker won the intermediate and high hurdles. Auburn's other winners were Joe Franklin in the 880, Bob Hicks in the 1000 and Tom Graves in the two-mile.

In response to the December 1979 Soviet incursion into Afghanistan, President Jimmy Carter announced in January 1980 that unless the Soviets withdrew from Afghanistan, the United States would boycott the Moscow Olympics. When the Soviets refused to withdraw their troops from Afghanistan, Carter announced the boycott in his State of the Union message

January 23, 1980: "I have notified the United States Olympic Committee that with Soviet invading forces in Afghanistan, neither the American people nor I will support sending an Olympic team to Moscow." The following day the House of Representatives voted 386–12 to support Carter's boycott.[4] The result was that the United States led a 61-nation boycott of the summer Olympics held in Moscow. "In the weeks before the trials, all the talk was whether the United States would boycott the Moscow Games. Harvey and I were driving to a meet, and I remember Harvey turning and saying to me, 'Coach, we're not going to Moscow are we?' I told him probably not. I thought about all the athletes who would be missing out on their one opportunity to go to the Olympics. Most athletes only get one chance to compete."

Most of the athletes on the United States Olympic Team strongly disagreed with the decision to boycott. Craig Virgin, now a sports broadcaster who in 1980 was a world record holder in the 10,000 meters and had a good chance to win the event, still has strong feelings about the boycott. "I may forgive, but I'll never forget. For me, it was just sad, because running was booming and I could have brought home a medal." When Jimmy Carter was asked if his Nobel Prize in 2002 vindicated his presidency, including the boycott, he replied, "I don't know of any decisions I made in the White House that were basically erroneous."

Despite the U.S. boycott, the 1980 Olympic trials were held as scheduled in Eugene, Oregon, in June. But the boycott meant that the trials were far less meaningful than usual. "The general feeling of the athletes and spectators was that this was just another track meet."[5] The mood at the trials was not helped by the rain, which fell for much of the event. Nevertheless, Auburn qualified four athletes for the 1980 Olympic team: Harvey Glance, Willie Smith, James Walker, and Stanley Floyd. Auburn dominated the 100-meter dash with Floyd and Glance finishing first and second. They beat such notables as Carl Lewis, Houston McTear, and Steve Riddick in the finals.

Stanley Floyd was becoming Auburn's most dominant sprinter. When Rosen recruited Floyd, he considered him Harvey Glance's heir-apparent. Floyd, a sprinter from Albany, Georgia, wasted little time adapting to the competition in the SEC. As a freshman, he won the SEC conference in the

100, placed third in the 200, and anchored Auburn's second-place 400-meter relay team. A few weeks later Floyd further demonstrated his dominance by winning the 100-meter dash at the 1980 NCAA championships. He topped off his extraordinary freshman year by qualifying for the 1980 Olympic team by winning the 100 meters, just edging out second-place finisher Harvey Glance.

One of the most exciting races in the trials was the 400 meters. Willie Smith, after an uncharacteristically slow start, surged and took the lead with just over 100 meters to go and controlled the race until the final 10 meters when Bill Green shot past to win by just a step. In the 400-meter hurdles, Auburn's James Walker ran one of his best races of the year but finished behind the great Edwin Moses. "Moses was the best runner I ever ran against," says James Walker. "He was in a class by himself."

Qualifying four athletes for the Olympics was a remarkable achievement for Auburn. No other university could boast so many qualifiers. On the strength of Auburn's success at the trials, and his team's four-straight SEC indoor championships, Rosen was named NCAA Coach of the Year in 1980. "The award was a real surprise to me. Things were happening so fast. I was enjoying the recognition. I think Coach Hutsell would have been pleased with the success I was having." The award put Rosen into consideration for an Olympic coaching position. "After I was named NCAA Coach of the Year, I began thinking that I may have a shot to be on the Olympic coaching staff. I didn't think I would be named head coach, but I thought I might have a shot as a manager for the team. But I felt time was running out as I wasn't getting any younger."

A FEW WEEKS AFTER the trials, Rosen was named head coach of the Eight Nations Meet held in Japan and China. The meet, scheduled by the U.S. International Olympic Committee, was an alternative competition to the Moscow Games for the American team. Most of the American athletes were ambivalent about going, as they were angry they couldn't complete in Moscow. Harvey Glance still recalls his feelings about missing the 1980 Olympics. "We thought that 1980 was our time. James, Willie, and I trained for four years to make the team. It wasn't fair that politicians kept us out of the Olympics. We would have made our mark. I had worked so hard to qualify. It still bothers me. It left scars." James Walker was also disillusioned about the boycott. "I had been training for the Olympics my whole time at Auburn. I was disappointed and angry at the same time. What good did the boycott do?" That feeling was shared by the majority of athletes in all of the Olympic sports. Rosen tried to keep the team focused on the competition, despite their disappointment. "My job was to be positive and keep the team focused. It wasn't easy because our team was angry that politics had ended their chance for going to Moscow to compete. Auburn had four athletes who qualified for the 1980 Olympics, and I hated to see them miss out on their opportunity."

It was during the Eight Nations meet that problems began to develop between Rosen and Stanley Floyd, Auburn's sensational freshman sprinter. Rosen had concerns about Floyd's attitude. "Stanley could be a selfish team-mate. He thought only about himself. He had Harvey Glance speed, but I wasn't sure if he had the mental makeup, the singular focus, to show up for every race." Floyd wanted to run only the 100 and 200. In an interview with *Sports Illustrated* in 1980, Floyd voiced his complaints about Rosen: "Before a meet he would go to the board and write out how many points he expected from each of us. Bam, bam, bam, bam. It was determined if you didn't get your points, you had failed. He always had me down for some ridiculous number like 18 in the conference meet." Rosen points out that Floyd in fact scored 18.5 points in the 1980 conference meet, exceeding his expectations. Floyd's other point of contention was he didn't want to run the 400. Rosen and Floyd began butting heads on this issue soon after Floyd arrived on campus. Rosen insisted that Floyd compete in any event necessary to help Auburn score points. At a team meeting beginning the 1981 season, Rosen told Floyd that if Auburn needed the points to win and Floyd refused to run the 400, then "they would part company."

During a pre-season meeting, Floyd saw Rosen had not added any sprinters, and he knew Rosen would continue to require him to pick up the slack by competing in the 400. Floyd wanted no part of it. Floyd knew Rosen well enough that he wouldn't change his mind. After the meeting Floyd came to Rosen's office and told him he was quitting but wanted to stay in Auburn and work out with the team. Rosen told him if he quit he couldn't work out with the team. Floyd became angry and said Rosen was being unfair since Harvey Glance was working out with the team and was no longer competing for Auburn. "I told Stanley that Harvey had paid his dues and deserved to work out with the team."

As an angry Floyd got up to leave he said sarcastically that he should take something with him so he could remember Auburn when he was running for another school. "I told Stanley he should take the chair he was sitting in since it was the same chair he had sat in all season complaining about me." After this confrontation Floyd decided to transfer to the University of Alabama. But Athletic Director Lee Hayley refused to release Floyd from his scholarship. "Coach Hayley was afraid that Floyd would end up playing football for Alabama. There was no way he was going to make it easy for Floyd to transfer to Alabama. He didn't want to see Floyd, with his speed, on the football field in a University of Alabama uniform."

Floyd transferred to the University of Houston and spent several years running for coach Tom Tellez, one of the most successful sprint coaches in the country. Floyd had a successful, but injury-ridden career at Houston. Leg injuries slowed down the speedster from Albany, Georgia.

Floyd's defection hurt Auburn. "Up 'til the time Floyd quit we had scored in nine-straight 100-meter dashes at the NCAAs. That streak ended when Floyd left." What bothered Rosen was not that Floyd had elected to leave—that happens with some frequency in collegiate athletics—but that he sabotaged the team by telling every recruit not to come to Auburn. "We lost a few guys because of Floyd. It set us back."

As a member of the USA Track and Field International Competition Committee Rosen attended their annual meeting in December 1981. It was then the 1984 Olympic coaching staff was selected. The nine-member staff was organized around a head coach with four assistants and a head manager with three assistants. In a surprise to Rosen, he was nominated for one of the assistant coaching positions. However, Rosen lost to Willie Williams, head track coach at the University of Arizona by a vote 15 to 9. A few minutes later, Rosen was selected as assistant manager. "I was delighted. To be on the staff for the Olympic team was a dream come true. Maybe they thought I had paid my dues because I was doing a lot of work with U.S. track and field. It was quite an honor. Williams was a terrific sprint coach. I roomed with him at different track and field events over the years. He was a gentleman, a quiet guy who had a lot of friends in the sport."

It had been 56 years since another Auburn coach, Wilbur Hutsell, was selected for the 1928 Olympic coaching staff. However when Rosen returned home to celebrate the holidays, little was said about his selection. But Rosen wasn't disappointed. He didn't expect any fanfare. "Auburn was not a track school. It didn't surprise me that very few knew I was on the Olympic staff. I just got back to work." At 52 years of age, Rosen had already achieved more than he ever could have imagined when, as a young man, he left Brooklyn on the train to Iowa.

8

NOT QUITE ENOUGH

(1982–1987)

"What was I thinking as I entered the Los Angeles Coliseum for the Games? If I had listened to my mother and stayed in Brooklyn I would have made a lot of money, but I would have been shoving around shmattes [rags] my whole life."

On January 14, 1982, Willie Williams, 41 years old and in his 13th season as head track coach at the University of Arizona, committed suicide. His body was found in a tool shed next to the university's track by one of his graduate assistants who said Williams had been despondent in the weeks prior. He left no suicide note. A 1962 graduate of San Jose State University and a highly regarded sprint coach, Williams was the first black head coach at any major university in any sport when he was hired at Arizona in 1969. Williams competed in the 1960 Olympics in the 200 and 400 meters and had been designated assistant coach for the 1984 United States Olympic team, thus making him a likely choice to become the head United States Olympic track coach for either the 1988 or 1992 Olympics. But it wasn't to be.

When the United States International Competition Committee met in December 1983, their main purpose was to select a coach to replace Williams. Sadness hung over the meeting. "Willie Williams was well liked in the coaching fraternity. I don't think anyone knew that he was having such problems. Everybody was shocked about Willie's suicide." After some discussion three coaches were nominated for the assistant coaching position: Erv Hunt, from the University of California; John Moon, coach at Seton Hall;

and Rosen. The three men were asked to leave the room so the selection committee could deliberate and vote. Rosen thought he had a good chance of winning because he had been second behind Williams in the original vote the year before. But he knew there were no guarantees. The men didn't have long to wait. Rosen was selected on the first ballot.

Larry Ellis from Princeton University was head coach and assigned Rosen the hurdlers, sprinters, and the 400-meter and 1600-meter relays. He and Rosen, both future Hall of Fame coaches, had known each other for two decades. Their partnership in the 1984 Olympics would turn out to be very successful.

BEFORE ROSEN BEGAN HIS preparation for the 1984 Olympic Games, he focused on Auburn track. Rosen was concerned about his team. He felt they had lost some of their competitive edge and were short on quality sprinters since the disgruntled Floyd transferred to the University of Houston.

Prospects for building the team had improved in 1982 when Harvey Glance told Rosen the good news that Bo Jackson had accepted a football scholarship to Auburn and that Coach Pat Dye had given him permission to compete in track and baseball. Jackson told Dye that he wouldn't come to Auburn to play football unless he was also allowed to play baseball and run track. Dye remembers their discussion. "I told Bo that it was all right with me if he participated in baseball and track as long as he was ready to play football in the fall, because it came first. I would have let him play any sport he wanted to make sure Bo came to Auburn."

As a senior at McAdory High School in Bessemer, Alabama, Jackson had won the 1982 high school state championship in the 100, the high hurdles, and the decathlon. He was just the high-profile recruit Rosen needed to make an immediate impact on the track program and to sway other track athletes to come to Auburn.

Despite Jackson's enormous potential, neither Rosen nor assistant coach Mike Muska (who followed Jerry Smith as Rosen's assistant after Smith left in 1977 to work for the Auburn University Alumni Association) had been involved in the effort to recruit him. "We stayed out of the way when the football coaches were recruiting an athlete unless they asked for our help.

You have to remember football is number one at Auburn, and I never wanted to get in their way when they were recruiting."

However, because of Jackson's interest in track, Dye asked Harvey Glance to help in the recruiting. Jackson had followed Glance's 1976 Olympic success and wanted to meet him. "I talked to Bo several times," Glance says, "and told him Auburn was a great place to go to school. He wanted to know about the track team and Coach Rosen. He loved hearing stories about the Olympics." (Glance's help in recruiting Jackson would become an important reason why Dye selected Glance to replace Rosen when Rosen retired in 1991.)

Jackson ran track at Auburn for two years, before leaving school to play professional football and baseball. Rosen: "Bo was easy to coach. He liked my workouts since I always undertrained sprinters. The lighter workouts matched his personality. His best event was the 60. His goal was to make the 1984 Olympic team. I told Bo that if he were serious about it he'd have to lose 30 pounds. He was too big to be an Olympic caliber sprinter. He just laughed when I told him that."

Jackson began the 1983 track season, his freshman year, running the sprints and the high hurdles. But the high hurdles in college track are three inches higher than in high school, and Jackson couldn't adjust to the height difference. "Bo kept breaking hurdles in practice. He just ran right through them as if he was running through a tackler on the football field. Replacing all those broken hurdles was breaking our budget!" By mid-year Rosen had seen enough and told Jackson to concentrate his efforts on the 60 and 100.

Jackson developed as a sprinter, and in 1984 he placed third in the SEC in the 60-yard dash and qualified for the NCAA indoor championships in Detroit. Rosen thought Jackson could place in the top six in the 60 and earn All American honors. The competition was fierce as Jackson ran against the likes of Tennessee sprinters Willie Gault and Olympian Sam Graddy. Jackson almost didn't get to run in the NCAA championships, however. "Bo missed the team flight. He forgot that Atlanta [Auburn's departure airport] was on Eastern Time and didn't make it to the gate. I thought Bo might miss the meet altogether, but he finally got to Detroit in time to run."

Despite running impressively in the early heats, Jackson didn't qualify for the finals in the 60. It was then he realized that he wouldn't qualify for the 1984 Olympic team. "That was a disappointment for Bo. He carried too much weight to compete at the elite level. I don't think Coach Dye would have liked Bo to lose about 30 pounds to become a better sprinter."

IN 1983 ROSEN HIRED Hal Cooper as his assistant coach to replace Mike Muska, who accepted a head coaching position at Northwestern University. Cooper assisted Rosen from 1983–91. Cooper, a former Auburn quarter-miler who had run for Rosen, immediately hit the recruiting trail and landed outstanding performers like Kevin Henderson, a 400-meter hurdler, and Boris Goins, a long jumper. Soon after Cooper was hired—he eventually became an ordained Baptist minister—he set up Bible study classes for some of the team members during road trips. The classes continued for about a year before another assistant coach and an athlete came to Rosen and complained about the classes. They said they felt pressured to attend. Rosen acted swiftly and told Cooper to discontinue the Bible studies during road trips, as they were divisive. Rosen told him Bible studies were fine as long as they took place away from the track and it was made clear to the team that attendance was voluntary. "I understood Mel's decision," Cooper says. "He had the interest of the team in mind." There was never any rift between Rosen and Cooper as a result of the cancellation of the Bible studies. Rosen considered Cooper one of his best assistants and would eventually lobby for Cooper to replace him when he retired. And it was Cooper who initiated a campaign in 1988 to have the track facility at Auburn be named the Hutsell-Rosen Track.

Rosen prepared for the Olympic Games by traveling to the 1983 World Track and Field Championships in Helsinki, Finland, to observe the U.S. team. The world championships would become known as the "Carl Lewis Games" as the venue provided the springboard for many of his future suc-cesses. Rosen expected many of the athletes on the world championship team to qualify for the Olympics. Stan Huntsman was head coach, and Russ Rogers assisted with the sprinters and relays in Helsinki.

Rosen wanted to observe the American 400-meter relay team of Emmit King, Willie Gault, Calvin Smith, and Carl Lewis as he was assigned to coach the relays in the 1984 Olympics. They didn't disappoint. Not only did they win the world championship, the team broke the world record, running a stunning 37.83. "I knew then our 1984 Olympic relay team would be dominant, barring injuries. I also decided after watching practices that if Emmit King made the Olympic relay team, he would lead off because he was lousy at taking the stick. I was not going to let him run in another position and jeopardize our chances in the Olympics."

Rosen also had a personal interest in the meet. Willie Smith, "the Long Island Express," was competing in the 1600-meter relay. Rosen had developed a close, almost paternal relationship with Smith, and he was worried about him. His star sprinter was having personal problems, and Rosen was trying to make sure Smith "didn't go down the wrong path." Rosen considered him one of the best curve runners in the country as long as he kept his focus. As the runners prepared for the race, Rosen watched Smith closely. Smith still retained that swagger great sprinters have before a big race. These intense moments just before a relay were Rosen's favorite part of the event.

At the gun, Michael Franks of the American team took an early lead. But by the time Smith took the baton from teammate Sunder Nix, the Americans were second just behind the highly regarded Russian team. Smith, who usually got stronger as a race progressed, began gaining on Nikolay Chernetskiy. Rosen waited for him to catch and fly past Chernetskiy. But, just as Smith maneuvered to take the lead, he stepped on the Russian's heel. Smith stumbled and fell. He jumped right up and tried to get back into the race, but unfortunately a German runner ran into Smith from behind, knocking him down again. He finally got up and finished his leg and handed off to Edwin Moses, who had no chance to catch the leaders. The American team finished a disappointing seventh place.

Dr. Tony Dailey, the U.S. team physician, went to the dormitory where Smith had secluded himself after the race, to make sure he wasn't injured. Smith was not injured, but Dailey was worried about his psychological condition. Smith was obviously very upset. Dailey found Rosen and told him he'd better go talk to Smith. Rosen found him sitting on his bed in the dormitory. He was inconsolable. As soon as Smith saw Rosen he cried out, "I just fell in front of a million people. Why does this kind of stuff always happen to me? It's not fair."

Rosen used his sense of humor to help Smith put things into perspective. "Willie you didn't fall down in front of a million people. It was more like a billion. You need to get your facts straight." Smith, familiar with his coach's sense of humor, regained his composure.

The American team won eight gold medals and 24 medals in total, more than any other country. Their strong showing in the World Championships served notice that the American Olympic team would be formidable in Los Angeles. "I felt we had a core group of runners like Carl Lewis, Calvin Smith, Emmit King, Greg Foster, and Edwin Moses who would make our Olympic team the strongest in the world. I just had to make sure that I provided them with the coaching support so they would win medals in Los Angeles."

THE 1984 OLYMPIC TRIALS took place in June at the Los Angeles Coliseum. Carl Lewis was the biggest name in men's track and field. He was expected to qualify in the 100, 200, and long jump. His goal was to win four gold medals, tying Jesse Owens's historic feat in the 1936 Olympics in Berlin. Rosen stated, "The hardest part for Carl was the mental aspect of getting prepared and not letting all the attention distract him. But Carl was the most talented and competitive athlete I ever coached. I knew he could win four gold medals."

Rosen and the 23-year-old Lewis were well acquainted. Years before, Rosen had seen Lewis compete in the long jump in several high school meets and knew immediately that the young man had enormous talent. Tom Tellez, coach at the University of Houston, and one of the most successful long jump coaches in the country, had won the recruiting battle and signed Lewis to a scholarship.

In 1979, Rosen was sprint coach when Lewis, then a high school senior from Willingboro, New Jersey, was selected to compete in the long jump and the 100 meters for the United States in the Pan American Games in Puerto Rico. On the morning of the long jump finals, Rosen noticed his young star wasn't at breakfast. With the starting time for the event fast approaching, Rosen rushed to the athletic dorm and ran up six flights of stairs to Lewis's room. Lewis was still in bed; he'd forgotten to set his alarm. Rosen woke Lewis telling him he had just 20 minutes to get to the stadium and if he was late to sign in he'd be disqualified. "He got up and casually put on his running gear. He showed no emotion, no worry. He told me, 'Don't worry, Coach, I'll get there.' It was then, seeing him keep his emotions in check, I knew Lewis had the talent and the composure needed to compete at the elite level."

In the Los Angeles trials, Lewis easily qualified for his three individual events. In the 100, after getting out even with his main competitor, Sam Graddy, Lewis turned on the power, and in mid-race he looked across the lanes and "imperiously flowed away" from the competition and then held his arms out wide as he glided past the finish line. Lewis stated confidently after the race, "I'm happy I won. I trained for this meet harder than anyone else." However, fans and sportswriters were critical of Lewis for slowing down at the end of the race and showboating. "Still smarting from that criticism," Lewis dominated the 200, beating second-place Kirk Baptiste by several yards.[1] Lewis next set his sights on qualifying for the long jump. Lewis, the world's number one long jumper, won by effortlessly jumping 28'7", and putting himself into position to win four golds.

Eight Auburn athletes competed in the track and field trials: Harvey Glance in the 100 and 200, James Walker and Forika McDougald in the 400-meter hurdles, Willie Smith in the 400 meters, Darren Council in the 200, Chris Fox in the 5000, Kevin Henderson in the intermediate hurdles, and Calvin Brooks in the 200 and 400.

Glance, Walker, and Smith were still upset about missing the 1980 Olympics in Moscow because of the U.S. boycott. Now they were trying to make the 1984 team. But the odds of making the Olympic team more than once are small. Rosen estimates that only about a third of Olympians in track and field make more than one Olympic team. The odds are even less for sprinters as their elite competitive lifespan is about three to four years. Rosen felt that Glance, who captained the 1980 track and field Olympic team, and Smith had a good chance of making the team, because even if they didn't place in the top three in their respective races they might qualify as alternates on the relay teams.

The remarkable Glance was attempting to make his third Olympic team, a feat never accomplished by an American sprinter up to that time. Glance, despite injuring a muscle during the 100, placed seventh, putting him in contention to be named as an alternate on the 400-meter relay. Smith placed sixth in the 400 finals, also high enough to qualify for an alternate spot on the 1600-meter relay. James Walker, running in the semifinal heat against Edwin Moses, placed fifth and didn't qualify for the finals. Chris Fox also just missed earning a spot in the 5000 by finishing in fifth place.

ESTABLISHING DISCIPLINE IS ONE of the most difficult challenges for an Olympic coach and requires finesse. "Olympic-caliber athletes are highly motivated, otherwise they wouldn't have gotten to the trials. But what's hard is to apply rules to such an accomplished group." Rosen was savvy enough to apply team rules selectively by weighing the interests of the athlete with those of the team. He knew that while the same rules apply to everyone on the team, you shouldn't treat all athletes the same. David Housel, former Auburn athletic director, feels one reason why Rosen was so successful as a coach was that he knew you had to individualize training and team discipline: "Because athletes come from so many different backgrounds, a coach has to take that into consideration. This is especially true when coaching African American athletes. Mel connected with them."

Hal Cooper, Rosen's long-time assistant coach, feels that Rosen's success stemmed from his ability to communicate. "He related to African American athletes. I think one reason was he was a minority himself. Being Jewish he knew what it felt like to be different. Because he wasn't Southern, he didn't carry the baggage a Southern-born-and-bred coach would have had coaching African American athletes. Mel's athletes knew his only prejudice was against laziness!"

Rosen's main concern during the three weeks between the trials and the Olympics was that his athletes stay healthy. A coach always walks a fine line between keeping athletes tuned up or overworking them and causing injury. Rosen scheduled five practices and three warm-up meets for the interim period. But Rosen and Carl Lewis had different expectations about attendance. When he went to Lewis to give him the team's practice schedule, Lewis balked at competing in any of the meets. "His dad was standing next to him. When I told Carl about our three o'clock practice for the following Monday, he told me his agent, Joe Douglas, had already scheduled several meets for him and he didn't have time to practice with the team. I knew that Douglas had him on a moneymaking tour. But that wasn't my concern. I told Carl that if he didn't show up at three o'clock on Monday I would pull him from the relay team. He looked surprised. I think he was sizing me up to see if I meant it. Before I said another word, Carl's dad said, 'Don't worry, Coach, Carl will be there. You can count on it.'"

Lewis's father was true to his word. On Monday afternoon at five minutes to three, Lewis pulled up with his dad in his brand-new Mercedes, dressed for practice. Rosen breathed a sigh of relief, as he didn't want to be known as the coach who benched Carl Lewis in the 1984 Olympics. Such an outcome wouldn't have been good for Lewis, and it certainly wouldn't have been good for Rosen.

Generally, Rosen wouldn't negotiate whether an athlete had to attend practice. His rule at Auburn was if you didn't practice, you didn't run in the meet. But Rosen compromised with Lewis. He excused Lewis from two of the three scheduled meets so he could return to Houston and work on his three other events with his coach, Tom Tellez. Lewis's 400-meter relay teammates Sam Graddy, Ron Brown, and Calvin Smith questioned whether Lewis was being allowed to set his own rules. Graddy complained, "If rules are set out for everybody on the team, it shouldn't exclude anybody."[2] Calvin Smith also voiced his displeasure, "I just feel all the athletes should be at the meets." Ron Brown was the most vocal. He met with Rosen to complain about the decision to allow Lewis to go to Houston and accused Rosen of playing favorites. Rosen told Brown that he wasn't playing favorites and if Brown had qualified for three individual events he would have let him go home and practice with his coach as well. "I knew they were going to be critical. But that is part of coaching. You have to stick to your philosophy and not worry about it."

THE LAST OF THE three Olympic warm-up meets was held in Sacramento. Rosen was obsessed about keeping his relay team healthy, so he told them to just stride through the race and not push too hard and focus on their exchanges. Rosen knew that something as minor as a pulled muscle could sideline a runner for six weeks or more. "Eighteen thousand fans showed up at the meet. I told the team to take it easy and just stride through the race. I took my place in the infield and hoped nobody would get injured. The temperature that night was cold, in the mid-forties, so I was worried about muscle pulls. At the gun, Sam Graddy came out of the blocks like a shot. Ron Brown, Calvin Smith, and Lewis glided around the track. Their exchanges were perfect. They didn't even break a sweat, and their time was just under the world record. I knew we could not only win Olympic gold in the 400-meter relay, but we could also break the world record."

A difficult and sometimes a contentious decision for coaches is the selection of the anchor for the relays. Most sprinters covet that position. They know when the anchor crosses the finish line with arms stretched overhead in victory he will be in the "money shot," the photograph everyone sees in the newspaper the next day. A savvy agent can convert that publicity into money—lots of it—for the athlete. There was no better agent at parleying gold medals into money than Joe Douglas, Carl Lewis's agent. It was estimated that by 1984 Lewis was earning close to a million dollars a year, and that figure would rocket higher if he could meet his goal of four Olympic gold medals. Douglas knew that if Lewis matched Jesse Owens's Olympic record, the "gold rush" would come after the Los Angeles Olympic Games.[3]

A memorable moment for Rosen in the Olympic training period came when President Ronald Reagan visited their training facility in Santa Barbara to wish the team good luck. When Reagan finished speaking and waved to the cheering crowd, he said as he was walking out. "Win one for the Gipper." One of the athletes standing next to Rosen asked, "Coach, what is a Gipper?"

THE SOVIET UNION, EAST Germany, and 13 other Communist-bloc countries boycotted the Los Angeles Olympics in retaliation for the U.S. boycott of the 1980 Moscow Olympics.[4] That didn't dampen the enthusiasm of the Olympic athletes or fans. The estimated television audience for the 23rd Olympiad was two billion viewers.

Rosen recalls the opening ceremonies and marching into the Olympic stadium filled with 95,000 cheering fans. "When I entered the stadium with all the teams, I saw thousands and thousands of fans waving American flags and flashing pictures. It was a fantastic sight. It was emotional. I couldn't help thinking of my mother and father. I think they would have been proud of me. I had come a long way from my days playing on the boardwalk in Brighton Beach!"

The security measures put in place in Los Angeles were extraordinary. Rosen listened to some of the athletes and coaches complain about what they considered excessive restrictions on their movement within the Olympic Village. But Rosen felt differently. He remembered the 1972 Munich Olympics and the 11 Israeli athletes who were massacred by Palestinian terrorists. It was something he thought about as he took his walk each morning with team psychologist Dr. Robert Nideffer.

Because of the limited number of field passes made available, Nideffer wasn't provided one to enter the Olympic stadium. As a consequence, he was unable to meet with the athletes at the practice track. Rosen tried to persuade his athletes to meet with Nideffer outside the stadium, but none took up the offer. So each morning Rosen and Nideffer walked, and he got the psychologist's ideas for reducing the stress of the athletes and how to positively motivate the team. "Walking with Nideffer was like having my own personal psychologist. It was the closest I ever got to being in therapy."

While almost 7,000 athletes from 141 nations competed in the 23rd Olympiad, most eyes were on Carl Lewis. Elliot Denman, sportswriter for the *Asbury Park News,* wrote that Lewis was the "crown jewel of the Olympic team" and seemed destined to "put his name right up there with Jesse Owens."[5] Because Rosen coached Lewis in three of his four events, he knew he would be held partly responsible if Lewis faltered. "I realized my Olympic career was on the line. If Carl didn't win four medals the finger-pointing would have been at me. But I wasn't worried about it. I thought the toughest medal was going to be the in the 400-meter relay since so many things can go wrong in that race."

Lewis won his four gold medals in the same events Jesse Owens had won in the 1936 Berlin Olympics. Lewis's first event was the 100 meters. While Rosen felt Lewis was the fastest runner in the field, any mistake, no matter how small, could cost him the victory. Rosen's concern, however, was quickly put to rest. Lewis won the 100 by coming from behind and beating teammate Sam Graddy by two meters. Lewis's second gold medal came in the long jump. Lewis, using only two of his allotted six jumps, easily won with a distance of 28'2". Lewis captured his third gold medal by leading the American team's sweep in the 200. Lewis took first while Kirk Baptiste and Thomas Jefferson placed second and third respectively. His time of 19.80 was a new Olympic record.

Despite his three golds, Lewis never became a crowd favorite. "I think one reason Carl had problems with the press and fans was that Douglas and his coach Tom Tellez kept him away from the press. They isolated Carl and wouldn't let him talk. Because of that Carl appeared arrogant. That didn't sit well with fans."

Trouble was brewing on the 400-meter relay team. Ron Brown and Calvin Smith thought Rosen would play favorites and use Glance in the finals, securing a medal for his friend. "I told them," remembers Glance, "that if they thought Coach Rosen would play favorites then they didn't know him very well. Any decision Coach made would be best for the team." Rosen decided he didn't want to use substitutes in the relay. He wanted his four best runners competing in every heat, practicing passing the baton.

Glance remembers his disappointment when he wasn't used in the relay. "I was disappointed. But I wasn't mad. Coach has integrity, and he did what he thought best for the team." Rosen: "I felt bad for Harvey not getting a gold medal, but we needed the practice handing-off, so I wanted the same four guys running all the heats. I made the right decision. We won the race and broke the world record."

The victory in the 400-meter relay gave Lewis his four gold medals. The American team of Sam Graddy, Ron Brown, Calvin Smith, and Carl Lewis broke the world record by running 37.83 seconds, beating second-place Jamaica by an incredible seven meters, with Lewis running an anchor lap of 8.4 seconds. As Lewis took his victory lap, he ran to the stands and took a large American flag from a spectator. Lewis ran with the flag as the Olympic crowd cheered. But not everyone liked the spectacle. Some felt that the flag had been planted before the race, and Lewis's victory lap with the flag was a staged marketing tool orchestrated by Lewis's agent, Joe Douglas. The *New York Times* wrote that Lewis's celebration was contrived, calculated. Rosen felt differently. "I didn't care whether Carl's celebration was contrived. It was good for our sport. Remember, we had boycotted the last Olympics, so any publicity about our team was a good thing. Lewis was a target of the press."

After Lewis collected his fourth gold medal, Ellis and Rosen met and discussed the possibility of running Lewis in the 1600-meter relay so he would have a chance of winning five gold medals. They decided running Lewis would be unfair to Ray Armstead, the runner Ellis and Rosen would have to replace. "Both Ellis and I felt that we could win the relay with Carl. He was an outstanding quarter-miler. But putting Lewis on the team at the last minute would have diminished his fifth gold medal and everything else he'd accomplished. We made the right decision."

ROSEN'S OLYMPIC COACHING SUCCESS was bittersweet. He felt bad for Harvey Glance. Glance, competing in his third Olympics, was an alternate on the 400-meter relay team, but was not eligible for a medal because he didn't run in the trials. Rosen didn't use Glance even in the early rounds because Tom Tellez had come to Rosen and asked him to run Carl Lewis in all the 400-meter relay heats because Lewis was booed during the long jump for only taking two of his six allotted jumps. Lewis had easily outdistanced his competition in his first attempt and scratched on his second attempt. He decided not to take any more jumps, so he could rest for his other events. Rosen: "Even though the fans and sportswriters didn't like his decision not to take all his jumps, it was a smart move by Carl. Fans didn't understand the physical and mental toll on Lewis competing in four events."

Rosen's substitution strategy was different for the 1600-meter relay. Rosen decided to use alternates in the early rounds, but with near-disastrous results. Sunder Nix, Ray Armstead, Antonio McKay, and Alonzo Babers made up the heavily favored U.S. relay team. Rosen substituted Walter McCoy and Willie Smith to rest Babers and McKay, the two fastest on the team, during the early rounds. That decision, however, almost led to the team's disqualification. When McCoy, running in the second slot, took the baton from Armstead, he stepped on the lane line. That is a rule violation and should have resulted in disqualification. McCoy knew he made a mistake. After he fouled, he "spent the rest of the race looking for the official to wave the red flag" disqualifying them.[6] The American team easily won the heat. But Italy and England protested, correctly charging the U.S. team stepped on the lane line. Head coach Ellis was beside himself with anger. "Ellis came running up to me yelling, 'How could McCoy cross the lane line? How could he make that kind of mistake?'" Both Ellis and Rosen, expecting the worst, waited for the result of the protest. Rosen thought they were going to be disqualified because McCoy did cross the line. "I guess because we were in our home field, the judges gave us a break and rejected the protest. We were lucky. It would have been devastating for the team if they were disqualified in the first round. We got a big break. It was a break for me too. A disqualification would have cost me the 1992 Olympic coaching job!"

The U.S. team, running from lane 8, dominated the finals. Alonzo Babers, running in the third position, gave the American team a big lead. He handed off to Antonio McKay who brought home the baton for an easy victory.

In track, alternates on relay teams had never before been awarded gold medals. Rosen tried to get the rule changed when he learned alternates on the American swimming relay teams earned medals as long as they swam in at least one heat during relay competition. Once Rosen returned to Auburn he petitioned the International Amateur Athletic Federation (IAAF) to change their policy and award gold medals to Willie Smith and Walter McCoy. Rosen spearheaded the five-month battle with the IAAF that resulted in the Olympic committee awarding gold medals to Smith and McCoy. Willie Smith received his medal in a ceremony at the East Tennessee Invitational track meet in front of his Auburn teammates. "Seeing Willie beaming after he got his gold medal made all the phone calls and letterwriting worth it."

THE USE OF PERFORMING-ENHANCING drugs had been a concern at the Los Angeles Games. Meet officials instituted new, stringent testing procedures to combat the problem. William Taylor wrote, "Most experts were aware that many of the American athletes were taking anabolic agents up to the 1984 Olympic Games."[7] Rosen and the track and field coaching staff had conversations about drug use on the team. They were concerned there might have been a handful of American athletes in the strength events using performance-enhancing drugs before the Olympics. In spite of the concerns about steroid use, all members of the U.S. Olympic track and field team passed the drug tests in Los Angeles.

Rosen wasn't naïve about the use of performance-enhancing drugs. He had witnessed a few athletes in international competition use them. In 1980 Rosen was coaching the U.S. team competing in the Eight Nations meet in Japan and China. One evening he went to the room of one of his shot putters to discuss the next day's training schedule. When Rosen entered the motel room, he immediately noticed pills spread out on a table. The athlete saw Rosen looking at the display of pills and said, "Coach, if you don't know what it is don't worry about it." Rosen has his ideas why drugs were taking over the sport. "Track athletes were able to earn large amounts of money in meets; there was more incentive to win anyway you could. Money was why so many athletes began using performance-enhancing drugs. Drug use was killing the creditability of our sport."

The 1984 American Olympic team won 174 total medals—83 were gold—easily outperforming second-place West Germany in the medal count. For Rosen, the 1984 Olympics couldn't have turned out better. Those athletes he coached won seven gold medals, 13 total medals, and set the world record in the 400-meter relay, the only world record by the track and field team. What was Rosen thinking about during the closing ceremony? He mostly thought about returning to Auburn and getting back to work. He also thought how lucky he had been to have learned the coaching business from two of the best, F. X. Cretzmeyer and Wilbur Hutsell.

A lingering question for many of the American athletes and coaches was what would have happened if the Soviet team and its 14 allies who boycotted had participated in the Games? Rosen felt that the United States still would have won more medals than any other country. "Even if the Soviets and the East Germans had been there Carl would have won all his events. But the Eastern bloc countries surely would have won medals in many of the strength events."

After the closing ceremonies, Rosen went directly home and didn't attend a victory breakfast with President Ronald Reagan or participate in the five-day national tour for medal winners and coaches. Rosen had scheduled his flight home for the day after closing ceremonies. Was he disappointed not to have participated in the festivities, which included a ticker-tape parade in New York City and an appearance at half time of the Dallas Cowboys-Pittsburg Steelers National Football League game? "I would have liked to have met President Reagan, but my flight was already made. I wanted to get home. I had been gone, like Moses in the desert, for 40 days and nights. It was time to get back to my real job and plan for track season."

Rosen's reception back home after his Olympic coaching success was muted at best. There were occasional interviews but, for the most part, few in Auburn knew Rosen had returned home as a successful Olympic assistant coach. When Rosen returned to work, he ran into Pat Dye, head football coach and athletic director. Dye asked Rosen how much money he made coaching the Olympics. Rosen, caught a little off guard, told him he earned $400—$10 dollars a day for 40 days of work. Dye looked at Rosen, shook his head in disbelief, and said, "You aren't going to get rich earning those wages!"

One unexpected benefit for Rosen was that, in his words, "he was a hot item at the Auburn Rotary Club!" As Rosen prepared to celebrate the holidays with his family, he received a Christmas card from Carl Lewis. Lewis, grateful to Rosen for helping him navigate his oftentimes difficult relationship with the press, wrote: "Mel, Many thanks for everything you did. We made it work together." Rosen was pleased he'd established a strong, positive working relationship with Lewis. That relationship would prove important when Rosen coached Lewis in the 1992 Olympics.

THE UNITED STATES INTERNATIONAL Competition Committee in 1985 named Rosen head coach of the 1987 United States track and field team for the World Championships in Rome. This assignment was considered the second most important coaching job in United States track and field, the most important being head Olympic coach. Rosen's appointment made him a primary contender for the 1992 Olympic head coaching position. But neither that nor the paltry salary of 10 dollars per day was on Rosen's mind as he prepared for the world championships.

When Rosen walked into the mess hall in Rome the first morning of competition, he knew he had a problem. The all-you-can-eat dining room for the athletes and coaches was open 24 hours. Rosen saw members of the American team with mounds of food piled on their plates. "All I could think about was a fat runner is a slow runner. I called a team meeting that afternoon and told them to not eat too much. I didn't want to see us eating ourselves out of a few gold medals."

Track and Field Magazine scheduled a "Meet the Coach" event for its 200 fans who followed the American team to Rome. When Rosen began discussing the 400-meter relay, an elderly lady in the back of the room raised her hand. "She asked me who I was going to run in the relay. I told her McRae, McNeill, Glance, and Lewis. She jumped up and asked 'What about Calvin Smith?' I told her he wasn't going to run. She informed me that Calvin Smith was the best curve runner in the world and insisted I run him in third position. I prayed we would win the race because if we didn't that little old lady was going to find me!"

During the 1970s and '80s, American track and field transitioned from amateurism to professionalism. This was a radical change in structure. For more than 100 years, amateurism defined the sport. The two major governing bodies that ruled track and field, the International Amateur Athletic Federation (IAAF) and the Amateur Athletic Union (AAU), "embraced amateurism as their central philosophy."[8] But many athletes felt that amateur rules and regulations were too confining and unfairly limited their earning power. Athletes aggressively fought for changes. As a result, "amateur rule reforms expanded compensation options to athletes and blurred the divide between amateur and professional."[9]

Rosen: "At first I didn't like the transition to a professional model. I was worried it would change the character of collegiate track and field. But as time went on, I came to understand that it was good for our sport. The increased opportunities for compensation made the professional life of the athlete longer and more productive." Money was a driving force in track and field by the mid-1980s. Elite athletes signed contracts with shoe companies or other sponsors who paid thousands of dollars for first-place finishes in major international meets. A case in point was Danny Harris, from Iowa State University, who was expected to challenge Edwin Moses in the 400-meter hurdles in the 1987 World Championships. Moses took a slight lead at the start and held off the surging Harris to win. After the race, Harris complained bitterly to Rosen that he won and demanded Rosen protest the result. Rosen and Harris asked the judges to look at the photographs of the finish. The photos showed that Moses had indeed won by just two one-hundredths of a second. "Harris was really disappointed. I found out why later. Had he won the race he would have earned $100,000 from one of his sponsors. The second-place finish was a bitter pill for him to swallow. It gives you a sense of the pressure the athletes were under to win and the amount of money at stake."

THE RACE EVERYONE WAS waiting to see at the 1987 World Championships was the 100-meter dash, which featured Carl Lewis and Canadian Ben Johnson. The two athletes, born just six months apart, couldn't have been more different from one another. Charlie Francis, Johnson's coach and trainer, was an Olympian sprinter himself, representing Canada at the 1972 Munich Olympics, when he was ranked fifth in the world.[10] Ben Johnson, compact and muscular, had grown up in poverty in Jamaica without a father. Aside from his extraordinary physical gifts, he was mentally tough with the ability of absolute concentration. Johnson was quiet, and kept his answers to questions from the press short and to the point. Lewis was lanky and had long, muscular legs. Where Johnson relied on his explosive strength to capture an early lead, Lewis combined his natural speed with extraordinary technical skills to win races in the last 40 meters. Lewis grew up with two parents, both coaches and educators, in a supportive, middle-class home. Both Francis and Rosen felt Lewis had complete faith in his ability but oftentimes came across as arrogant. Lewis was extraordinary disciplined and kept to his regular training routine without fail.

Adding to the tension in the race was that the two men had, since the 1984 Olympics, developed an intense dislike for one another, which made Lewis's earlier losses to Johnson in 1985 and 1986 in the 100 meters all the more difficult for him to swallow. When Lewis and Johnson lined up for the start of the 100 meters, Rosen was confident Lewis would win. He was healthy and was posting some of his fastest times. But winning would not be easy. Along with the formidable Johnson, Lewis lined up against Raymond Stewart from Jamaica and Linford Christie from Great Britain, both fast, experienced competitors. But Rosen wasn't looking at Stewart or Christie, he couldn't take his eyes off Johnson. Rosen hadn't seen Johnson since 1983 at a meet in Colorado Springs and was shocked to see how much stronger he appeared. Johnson, always a muscular man, had put on even more muscle.

At the sound of the gun, Johnson exploded out of the blocks and took an early lead. Johnson always used his start to dominate competitors from the beginning of a race. Lewis began gaining speed after the first 40 meters. Rosen expected Lewis to catch Johnson around the 70-meter mark. But Johnson found another gear, and Lewis couldn't catch the blazing Johnson. The race wasn't even close. Johnson won going away. "As soon as Johnson crossed the finish line well ahead of Carl, I knew something wasn't right. I remembered what Charlie Francis said to me in Colorado Springs in 1983. He said they were going to get Lewis soon. It was an odd thing for Francis to say, and he was so emphatic about it, that's why I remembered it." It would not be until the following year at the 1988 Seoul Olympics that Rosen would finally put the pieces together when Johnson, after failing a drug test, admitted using anabolic steroids since the early 1980s given him by his coach and physician Charlie Francis. "Carl suspected Johnson was using steroids all along but never made any public accusations because prior to 1988 Johnson never failed a drug test."

Rosen encountered another type of cheating at the 1987 World Championships. Larry Myricks, a long jumper from Mississippi College, held third place as the final long jumper, an athlete from Italy, prepared for his final attempt. Rosen saw the Italian's effort was well short of Myricks's mark. Rosen congratulated Myricks on his apparent third-place finish.

A few minutes later, however, an Italian judge posted the jump of his countryman as several inches longer than Myricks's jump. Rosen saw the posting and became enraged. He filed a formal protest, but the rules committee ruled against Myricks and awarded third place to the Italian. Rosen, undeterred, continued protesting to meet organizers for several weeks after the close of the World Championships. His persistence paid off. Myricks was finally awarded the third-place medal several months later. "It was the first time I encountered blatant cheating at any level of our sport. I think this was the maddest I ever was at a track meet. I have seen officials make mistakes, big ones, but they were mistakes. The situation at Rome was a clear case of cheating. The judge was suspended, and Myricks got his third-place medal."

BEING NAMED ASSISTANT COACH for the 1984 Olympic team and head coach of the 1987 World Championship team would have been enough to cap a career for many coaches, but not for Rosen. "There is one thing you need to know about Brooklyn Jews from our era," says Sol Saporta, Rosen's high school friend. "Whatever success you attain, it's never enough. Jews are always striving to fit in." Saporta was saying that for American Jews coming of age in the 1930s and 1940s, success was one avenue for gaining acceptance into the larger American community. But the road to acceptance can be long and bumpy.

Once back home in Auburn, the 56-year-old Rosen assessed his career. He had already achieved more than he thought possible when he began coaching. He had seen many of his coaching colleagues come and go over the years; some retiring and others moving to more lucrative business opportunities. Sitting in his second floor office inside Eaves-Beard Memorial Coliseum, surrounded by memorabilia acquired over a lifetime of coaching, he knew the fire to compete was still there. His dream, which began as a youngster on the streets and playgrounds in Brooklyn, was to be head Olympic coach. And with his stubborn resolve, he decided to stay in the game because as much as he'd accomplished, it still wasn't quite enough.

DREAMS COME TRUE

THE BARCELONA GAMES, 1992

"I saw all the Orthodox Jews with their black hats and coats writing their prayers in Hebrew. I hoped God would read mine in English."

The 1988 Olympic Games were held in South Korea, and despite having been an assistant coach at the 1984 Games and head coach at the 1987 World Championships, Rosen was not on the coaching team in Seoul. He was watching the 1988 Games from his home in Auburn while pondering whether time was running out for him to be named head Olympic coach for track. After all, he was 61 and might be considered too old by some members of the selection committee. The previous three Olympic track coaches, Jimmy Carnes (1980), Larry Ellis (1984), and Stan Huntsman (1988) were all younger than Rosen when they were selected.

The United States had never had a Jewish head Olympic track and field coach, and Rosen wanted to be the first. He had a small concern that anti-Semitism might come into play. While he never experienced direct discrimination in his collegiate coaching career, Rosen felt the head Olympic coach selection might be another matter. He remembered his high school friends warning him he would face anti-Semitism if he moved to the South. But Rosen had never worried about it. "It was interesting to me how Mel was able to assimilate into the coaching profession without any real problems," says Sol Saporta, Rosen's friend from his old neighborhood in Brooklyn. "Mel is the ideal assimilated Jew. Everyone likes him. He doesn't have the hard edges some New York Jews have. I am sure most people in Auburn and his coaching colleagues never think of Mel's Jewishness. It is not something

Mel displays." Kenny Howard, Auburn's athletic trainer from 1948–75 and assistant athletic director from 1975–80, observed Rosen's ability to fit into a small-town Southern environment. "Rosen blended. He wasn't one of those Orthodox Jews wearing a yarmulke all the time. He was quiet about his religion."

As he neared retirement age, Rosen felt his best and last chance to be head Olympic coach was for the 1992 Games in Barcelona, but his old friend Russ Rogers was the assistant coach in charge of sprints in Seoul, which would make him the obvious choice for head coach in 1992. "Russ was one of the best sprint coaches in the country, and he was known for his relay teams. I figured he was the likely choice for Barcelona. I thought maybe my time had passed."

Ironically, the disastrous outcome of the 400-meter relay in Seoul played a significant role in catapulting Rosen into prime contention for the Olympic track and field head coaching position in Barcelona.

Both American relay teams were heavily favored to win gold medals in Seoul. Rosen knew how Rogers normally prepared his relay teams, so he was surprised when in the early rounds of the 400-meter relay Rogers substituted freely, trying to win medals for all six qualifiers. Rosen thought the four fastest runners—Lee McRae, Joe Deloach, Calvin Smith, and Carl Lewis—who would run in the finals needed as much practice as possible handing off the baton. Rogers's wholesale substituting limited their practice time under racing conditions.

In the semifinals of the 400-meter relay, the American team pulled away from the field, and by the end of the third leg held a 15-meter lead. Rosen watched on television as Calvin Smith prepared to hand the baton to anchor Lee McNeill, who was substituting so Carl Lewis could prepare for the long jump finals. McNeill began his run, with his hand thrust back to receive the baton from Smith. Rosen saw at once that they were having trouble with the exchange. "I saw Smith miss McNeill's hand on his first handoff attempt. Because they had such a big lead, McNeill could have stopped running and just taken the baton from Smith and still qualified. But McNeill panicked. He kept running and began waving his hand back and forth trying to find the baton. That was his mistake. He should have held his hand still and let Smith complete the exchange. I saw McNeill run past the 20-meter exchange zone without the baton and that's a disqualification." When Smith and McNeill botched the exchange, Rogers was no longer a contender for head coach at the 1992 Games; he would have to take the responsibility for the disqualification. That is what happened to Stan Wright, an assistant in charge of the sprints and relays in the 1972 Olympics. Wright had somehow gotten the wrong competition schedule for the 100-meter semifinals. As a result he brought Eddie Hart and Ray Robinson to the track too late to check in with officials for their race; both were disqualified. Hart and Robinson had broken the world record in the United States Olympic trials and were expected to be part of an American sweep in the 100 meters in Munich. Wright's mistake cost him the 1980 Olympic head coaching job.[1]

IN 1989 ROSEN WAS selected for the third time to coach the American track and field team competing in the Maccabiah Games in Israel. Each time he coached in the Maccabiah Games, Israeli sports officials asked him to emigrate to help develop their track and field team. "The Israelis were trying to build all their athletic programs by recruiting Jewish coaches and athletes from all over the world. During the 1980s, they recruited Jews from the Soviet Union. As much as I enjoyed going to Israel, I never seriously considered staying. I don't think Joan and the children would have liked living in Israel."

A few days before the competition, Rosen and his team took a tour of Israel. They visited Masada, the most popular tour site of visiting Jews and the symbol of Jewish survival, and the Western Wall, considered the holiest of the Jewish sites.[2] "To see Jews from all over the world praying together at the Wall—and the contrast between the ultra Orthodox and the Reform Jews from the United States—was an emotional experience for me." When Rosen stood at the Western Wall, he followed the custom of inserting a written prayer or petition, into its cracks. Rosen wrote two prayers. His first asked for good health for everyone in his family. In his second, he asked to be named Olympic head coach. "I thought, why not, what could it hurt? When I walked away from the Wall, I figured I had done everything I could do to be named head Olympic coach."

The selection of the head Olympic track coach took place in November

At the Western Wall in Jerusalem, 1989.

1989 at the International Competition Committee (ICC) meeting in Washington, D.C. Rosen knew he was a contender. While he didn't lobby for the position, two of his long-time coaching friends did on his behalf. Dean Hayes, coach of Middle Tennessee State University, and Steve Simmons, from the Acusplit Track Club and former Oregon State University coach, had been working behind the scenes making Rosen's case.

Five candidates were nominated by the selection committee: Tom Tellez, Sam Bell, Harry Groves, Berny Wagner, and Rosen. They were asked to leave the room as the committee deliberated and voted. "We were out of the room for about an hour or so. We talked about everything except the head coaching job." When the nominees were escorted back into the room Hayes gave Rosen the "thumbs up" sign, and he knew then he was the 1992 Olympic head track and field coach. "After a burst of excitement, all I could think of was whether I really wanted the job. I knew that drugs would be an issue, and I wasn't sure I wanted to be involved with all that. But after this fleeting thought, I couldn't wait to get started preparing. It was a dream come true. I had confidence I could do a good job as head coach. It was something I worked hard for my entire career."

Rosen also thought about how good luck probably played some role in his selection. Three coaches whom he considered giants in the profession never got the opportunity to serve as head Olympic track and field coach. Irv Mondschein, who led track at the University of Pennsylvania from 1979–87 and was a former Olympian himself, "was a master at motivating his athletes. He was competitive but always played by the rules. He was one of my few Jewish counterparts." Bill Dellinger, head coach at the University of Oregon for 25 years, was, in Rosen's words, "a great coach and administrator; an innovator in the coaching profession. He led Oregon to five NCAA titles." Tom Tellez, who led the University of Houston for 22 years, was "the master technician in the sprints and jumping events. He applied the science of movement to his coaching."

Those three worthy men had not had the good fortune to be chosen. Rosen had, and he was resolved to take every advantage of his opportunity to lead the United States Olympic team.

A few days after Rosen returned to Auburn, he received a congratulatory letter from Bob Paul, the communications director for the United States Olympic Committee. Paul wrote: "Just remember, Mel, there will be 260 million people watching your every move." Unfazed, Rosen wrote back: "There might be 260 million people watching, but in Auburn there will be 20,000 people who won't know I left town!"

In the months before he was selected Olympic coach, Rosen had decided that if selected, he would retire from Auburn so he could devote full time to the Olympic coaching responsibilities. He didn't want anyone to think he wasn't giving 100 percent as Olympic coach. He also knew his Auburn athletes deserved a coach who was completely focused on them, and he felt he couldn't provide them his undivided attention while also preparing for the Olympics. A few days after he was named Olympics head coach, Rosen met with Auburn associate athletic director Oval Jaynes and told him he was stepping down as head coach but would continue as an instructor in the physical education program.

Rosen never discussed retiring with Joan. When Rosen told her of his decision, she was shocked. "I thought it was a decision that I had to make by myself. That's why I didn't discuss it with Joan or anyone else."

Joan said, "I couldn't believe Mel retired from coaching. He didn't discuss it with me. If he had I would have told him he was too young to leave coaching. I thought Mel made a mistake."

But Rosen had no second thoughts. His 28 years as head coach at Auburn was enough. He no longer wanted to put in the long hours of recruiting necessary to run a successful collegiate track program. Also, the ever-increasing number of rules imposed by the NCAA was becoming overwhelming. "By the time I retired, the NCAA Rule Book was as thick as the New York City telephone directory. I had had enough."

It was time to let a younger coach take over the responsibility. After a short search in which Rosen played no part, Auburn Athletic Director Pat Dye selected Harvey Glance to replace Rosen. Glance's first move was to ask Rosen

if he would serve as an unpaid assistant coach. Rosen, as his predecessor Wilbur Hutsell had, accepted without hesitation.

Rosen, after 28 seasons as head coach, turned over the reins to Harvey Glance in 1991. Glance is wearing the Olympic gold medal that he won at Montreal in 1976 (courtesy of Auburn University Photographic Services).

THE 1992 OLYMPIC TRIALS took place in the sweltering heat and humidity of summertime New Orleans. Temperatures hovered around 90 degrees all 10 days of the competition. The trials produced no record performances, but the competition was as fierce as it had ever been.[3] The biggest surprises in the trials were Dan O'Brien's failure to qualify for the decathlon and Carl Lewis's sixth-place non-qualifying finish in the 100 meters.

O'Brien's difficulty was particularly unexpected. After the first day of competition in the decathlon, O'Brien, the world champion in the event and heavily favored to win gold in Barcelona, was well ahead of the field and on his way to registering a world record performance. Rosen remembers what happened when he walked into the stadium on the second day of the decathlon to check on O'Brien during the pole vault competition. "Bill Buckhalter, a sportswriter from the *Orlando Sentinel,* came running up to me and said, 'Fred Samara [decathlon coach] just jumped off the top of the stadium.' As soon as he said that I knew something had happened to O'Brien. He told me O'Brien had no-heighted and didn't qualify for the Olympics. I couldn't believe it." O'Brien had passed in the earlier rounds and then failed to clear his opening height in the pole vault. As a consequence, O'Brien finished a distant 11th place and didn't qualify for Barcelona.

Carl Lewis, on the other hand, had been ill. He developed a sinus infection just before the trials that spread to his thyroid, liver, and kidneys. As a result, he finished sixth in the finals, which was not good enough to qualify for the 100-meters but was good enough to be named an alternate on the 400-meter relay behind qualifiers Dennis Mitchell and his Santa Monica Track Club teammates, Mark Witherspoon, Leroy Burrell, and Mike Marsh. Lewis did qualify in the long jump finishing second behind his main competitor and world record holder Mike Powell. After the trials, Lewis came to Rosen and told him he didn't want to run as an alternate in the 400-meter relay, so he could focus exclusively on the long jump. Rosen was surprised with Lewis's decision but named James Trapp, from Clemson University, to replace Lewis as alternate for the relay.

Rosen was disappointed that O'Brien and Lewis didn't qualify in their individual events because both were potential gold medalists. Despite these disappointments, Rosen liked the American system of requiring athletes to qualify at the trials for the Olympic team. "Great Britain uses their Olympic trials to qualify only two places for each event. The coaching staff selects the athlete for the third spot. The American system is by far the best. There are no politics involved, and you qualify the best performers at the trials. But it is a system that produces surprises." Despite O'Brian's failure to qualify, Rosen felt good about the team, saying to the press "If we run as well as we ran in the trials we'll win more medals than any other country."[4]

Rosen traveled with his Olympic team to Narbonne, France, about a two-hour drive from Barcelona, for the three-week pre-Olympic training period. Rosen considered his track and field team the most talented ever assembled. His goal—tricky to accomplish—was to supervise workouts making sure the athletes stayed tuned up but uninjured.

Rosen called a team meeting on the first day of training camp. As he stepped to the podium and looked out at his team, he saw that many of his elite athletes were absent. They were competing in various track meets in Europe to earn prize money. Rosen, uncharacteristically emotional, told those present to focus on winning events, not world record performances. He said, "Records can always be broken, but championships will always last." He also told them that he wanted to place a finalist in every event, a feat no American Olympic team had ever accomplished. Steve Plasencia, a distance runner who competed in the 10,000 meters, came up to Rosen afterwards and told him it was the most stirring speech he had ever heard. One of Rosen's assistant coaches asked how he was able to be so relaxed under so much pressure. Rosen joked that he had bought a little cabin in the mountains around Barcelona, and if they lost he was going to sneak there and hide out the rest of his life.

Rosen told colleagues and friends before leaving for Barcelona that they would know the team was doing well if his name was not mentioned in the press. He had learned in his long career that the press doesn't want to talk to you if your team is winning, but if you are losing reporters want your story. For much of the Olympics, Rosen managed to keep his name out of the press. To maintain a low profile, he avoided the mixed-areas, spaces reserved for the press to interview athletes and coaches. Rosen was content to let medal winners interview without him. He felt it was their time for the spotlight. In fact, he never tried to track down and talk to any of the athletes who won medals; instead, he counseled those who lost. "I sought out the athletes who didn't place. The winners didn't need me to congratulate them. They had the press and their agents to do that. I was more concerned with those who gave their best effort but lost. They needed me more."

More than 10,000 athletes from 172 nations, without a single country boycotting, participated in the Barcelona Olympic Games. Rosen brought approximately 70 athletes to Barcelona, by far the largest track and field team in the competition. The American policy was to bring any athlete who qualified, even if they had little or no chance of winning a medal. "We wanted to give our athletes an Olympic experience even if they weren't going to place in the finals. Our approach was costly but was an investment in the future."

ROSEN CALLED A COACHES' meeting on the day the team arrived in Barcelona. He remembered what happened to Stan Wright in the 1972 Olympics. He made up his mind it wasn't going to happen to him or any of his assistants. He told his assistant coaches to escort their athletes to the stadium to make sure they got to their events on time. To determine how long it took to get from the Olympic Village to the stadium, Rosen assigned one coach to take a taxi, another to take the shuttle bus, and he walked the distance. The shuttle bus took 20 minutes. Rosen established the rule that coaches would leave for the Olympic stadium two hours and 20 minutes before an event began. Rosen figured a two-hour cushion would be enough should there be trouble with the shuttle bus.

While no American track and field athlete was late for check in and always had enough time to properly warm up before their event, Switzerland's Werner Günthör, the 1991 world champion in the shot put and the favorite to win in Barcelona, wasn't so lucky. Rosen sat near Günthör on the shuttle on the final day of the shot put competition. After 20 minutes, Rosen looked out the window and didn't see any of the landmarks he had seen during previous trips to the stadium. Rosen saw that the 300-pound Günthör was getting nervous about how long the trip was taking. The driver,

Preparing for opening ceremonies of the XXIII Olympic Games, 1992.

who was from Seville and was making his first trip from the Olympic Village to the stadium, was hopelessly lost. When the athletes on the bus realized their predicament, panic set in and several started screaming obscenities in various languages. In a fit of rage, Günthör jumped from his seat and tried to wrestle the steering wheel from the driver. After a brief struggle, the driver convinced Günthör to sit down so he could get directions to the stadium. When Günthör finally arrived at the stadium, he didn't have enough time to warm up and failed to place in the shot put.

As a result of Günthör's misfortune, Americans Mike Stulce and Jim Doehring took first and second place in the shot put. Neither had attended the training camp in Narbonne. Stulce and Doehring came to Barcelona only a couple of days before the shot put competition. "The first time I saw them was when they were spinning in the circle competing. As soon as they were awarded their medals they left the Olympic Village, and I never saw them again! The head Olympic coach is sometimes more an administrator than a coach."

Despite Rosen's fear that performance-enhancing drugs might be a major problem in the Olympic Games, only five athletes tested positive out of the more than 1,800 drug tests administered. American hammer thrower Jud Logan, who finished a surprising fourth place, tested positive for the drug Clenbuterol. Logan's fourth place was the highest finish for an American hammer thrower since Hal Connolly won a gold medal in the event in 1956. Logan's disqualification and subsequent four-year ban from the sport was a major disappointment to Rosen. He considered Logan's high finish a breakthrough performance. "I thought he would become a great ambassador for the sport and a force for increasing interest in the event. But the positive drug test took care of that. Even then, the use of performance-enhancing drugs was killing our sport."

Rosen's Olympic-sized troubles began in the days leading up to the relay competitions. First, Carl Lewis created bad feelings among members of the team by changing his mind about competing in the 400-meter relay and attended every practice. His presence was disruptive. As soon as James Trapp saw Lewis at practice, he concluded he had no chance of running and told Rosen he was going home to Clemson and get ready for football practice. Trapp's departure added to speculation that Rosen was determined to run Lewis. Team members were convinced Rosen and Lewis had made a pact and Rosen would figure a way to run Lewis. Dennis Mitchell went to the press and complained that Rosen was planning to run Lewis even though he didn't qualify in the 100-meters, and that he was lying to them about his intentions. Rosen responded by saying that he would not make up his mind who was going to run until 48 hours before the event. "Carl never tried to pressure me into naming him to run the relay. I respected him for that." One reason was that Lewis didn't want to bump his friends, Mike Marsh, Mark Witherspoon, or Leroy Burrell, from the team.

Mitchell was particularly critical, saying that Rosen was "scheming" to get Lewis on the team. Rosen: "That couldn't have been further from the truth. I was not going to use Carl unless someone got hurt and couldn't run. But Mitchell didn't believe anything I said."

As fate would have it, on the day of the 100-meter semifinals Witherspoon, who was running alongside teammates Marsh and Burrell, ruptured his Achilles tendon. The injury knocked him out of the 400-meter relay finals, and Rosen then named Lewis as his replacement.

Rosen's troubles weren't over, however. The tension between Mitchell and Lewis continued to escalate. The major point of contention was that both wanted to run anchor. Mitchell told Rosen since he'd won the 100-meter trials that he deserved to be anchor. Neither Mitchell nor Lewis would back down. During the three scheduled relay practices, they bickered. Rosen tried to keep the two apart as much as possible, but emotions were getting more heated. Harry Groves, an assistant coach who helped Rosen with the relay, recalled the deteriorating situation: "Dennis wanted to anchor because it meant his sponsors would give him more money. Lewis didn't need the money." It was, according to Groves, "just a matter of pride" that Lewis wanted to anchor the relay.

Lewis's and Mitchell's relationship became so rancorous that Groves urged Rosen to make the call quickly who was to run the anchor before things "exploded." Rosen acted immediately telling both Mitchell and Rosen, "Carl, you're going to run anchor. Dennis, you're going to run the third leg because you are the best turn runner in the world and if you guys don't want to do it, get on the plane and get the heck out of here. I will substitute for you both!"

Rosen's rationale for selecting Lewis to anchor was straightforward: "He was the fastest man in the world and when the other anchors looked across the track and saw Carl, they would be scared out of their wits."

Rosen's threat solved the problem. Both men came to him apologetically. "Their attitudes changed when they realized that I would have replaced them both if the fighting continued. I didn't want to do that, but I had to do something to get things back on track. The way things were going, we were going to lose the relay because of the hard feelings."

Two hours before the finals in the 400-meter relay, Mitchell came to Rosen and told him the team was going to the practice track and work on stretching the 20-meter exchange zones at full speed. Rosen couldn't believe what Mitchell was telling him. "I screamed at Mitchell, are you crazy? You guys are going to risk injury at this point. I told him and the rest of the team to run three-quarter speed through the exchanges." Rosen had preached to the team all along to run the race conservatively and not worry about breaking world records. Rosen wanted gold medals. In his view the gold medal count was the important measuring stick for success, not records. As Rosen told *Sports Illustrated* writer Kenny Moore, "The name of the game in the Olympics is to be careful and win."[5]

Rosen sat in the stands next to Barbara Jacket. Jacket, head women's coach at Prairie View, was head coach of the women's Olympic track and field team. As the teams prepared for the finals of the 400-meter relay, Rosen tried to keep his emotions in check. "I was relieved when it was finally race time. We had the most talent, but because the chemistry among team members left something to be desired, I wasn't sure about the outcome." Rosen knew that in the 400-meter relay there is a thin margin for error; one small mistake with any of the exchanges could result in a disqualification.

Finally, the gun sounded for the start of the race. Rosen, hearing the collective roar of the 65,000 fans, rose in his seat to get a better view. Marsh and his Nigerian competitor edged ahead of the field. "Marsh did his job. He had a great start. He held his own, and the exchange between him and Burrell was perfect." In fact, *Sports Illustrated* described their exchange as "slick, safe, and swift." Rosen had selected Burrell to run the second leg because he didn't see well from one eye "and is best on the straightaway."[6] By the end of Burrell's leg, the American team was still battling Nigeria for the lead. Once Mitchell took the baton from Burrell, he shot ahead of the field. As Rosen had said, Mitchell was the fastest curve runner in the world. Mitchell gave the American team a three-meter lead. When he successfully handed the baton to Lewis, Rosen knew the race was over. So did Lewis. Just before Lewis took the baton, he looked over at the other anchors and would say after the race, "I could feel the energy dying out in the other anchors. It was obvious we were going to win."[7] Lewis, who just two days earlier had beaten world record holder Mike Powell to win the long jump, took command of the race and broke the spirits of the other anchors. Nobody was going to catch the fastest man in the world. Lewis extended the lead to about seven meters as he crossed the finish line. Rosen looked up to the electronic score board and saw they had run the race in 37.40 seconds, a new world record.

As soon as Lewis crossed the finish line the celebration began. A jubilant Lewis and his teammates jogged a victory lap arm-in-arm. Mitchell and Lewis were particularly demonstrative, hugging, patting each other on the back. Observing from his seat in the stands, Rosen turned to Barbara Jacket and said, "Look at them. Mitchell hasn't talked to Carl all week. Now he jumps into his arms. You'd think they were one big happy family!"

ROSEN STAYED IN THE stands and let his victorious team talk to the press without him. He wanted to prepare himself for the 1600-meter relay. "The pressure with the relays in the Olympics is that American fans expect us to win both. If you don't, fans want to know what happened. Second place won't do in the relays." In the 1600 relay, there was another controversy, regarding who would run on the 1600-meter relay. This dust-up was sparked by a U.S. loss in the 1991 world championships when Great Britain's Kriss Akabusi passed world 400 champion Antonio Petteigrew at the end of the anchor leg. After watching that outcome, Rosen decided that he wanted Michael Johnson to run the relay in the Olympics. But the U.S. rules required the 1600 relay team to be taken from the top finishers in the 400 meters at the trials. The problem for Rosen was that Johnson did not run in the 400 at the trials; he had wanted to focus on the 200 meters. Thus, according to the rules, he wasn't eligible for the relay. But soon after the 1991 world championships, the ICC had empowered Rosen to select anyone from the team to compete in the relay. Danny Everett had been vocal that it was "insulting to the rest of the 400 men to imply that we could not win without Michael Johnson and weren't intelligent enough to see that this policy was for Michael Johnson alone."[8]

These hard feelings were carried over to Barcelona as the team began its preparation for the race. Rosen was criticized in the press by members of the Santa Monica Track Club in the week leading up to the 1600-meter finals. This time the difficulty was between Everett and his Santa Monica teammates and Michael Johnson. The Santa Monica group felt Michael Johnson shouldn't run since he hadn't qualified in the 400-meters in New Orleans. Trying to counter the dissension and curb the team's criticism of him, Rosen called a team meeting a week before the qualifying heats were scheduled to begin. Assistant coach Bill Moultrie from Howard University opened the meeting by telling the team members how honored he was to be working with them. Before Moultrie could finish, Everett interrupted, saying, "Cut the bullshit. Just tell us who is running and in what order." The startled Moultrie just looked at Rosen, not knowing how to respond. Rosen immediately took over for his stunned assistant coach and laid out his plans for the relay. He told them Andrew Valman, Darnell Hall, Johnson, and Steve Lewis were going to run in the semifinals. In the finals it would be Everett, Quincy Watts, Johnson, and Lewis. Upon hearing Rosen's plans, Everett and Lewis exploded, saying that Michael Johnson hadn't qualified in the 400 meters in New Orleans so how could Rosen select him to run in the relay? Steve Lewis weighed in on the possible exclusion of Valmon, saying, "Andrew earned a spot on the team. If he wants to run he should run. If Johnson runs, I definitely oppose that."[9]

Rosen: "I told them the rule had changed and I had the authority to use anyone in the relay as long as they were members of the Olympic team. So it was my decision who would run." Everett continued arguing with Rosen, now saying he didn't want to run in the early rounds, only in the finals. After sitting quietly through the meeting, Johnson finally had had enough and jumped up and dramatically pointed to each of his five teammates in the room and said, "Don't forget I beat your ass, your ass, your ass, your ass and your ass. I'm the fastest guy in the room. I'm going to run the relay."

The meeting ended with Everett and Lewis storming out of the room and going to the press complaining about Rosen's selection of Johnson for the relay. Everett accused Rosen of playing favorites by selecting Johnson because both were paid by Nike to be sponsors. According to Everett, it was all about the money, that Rosen was pressured by Nike to select Johnson. "Everett's accusations were ridiculous. I made $1,000 from Nike. Why would I sell my soul for such a small amount of money? It was pure jealously. Everett, Lewis, and some of the others didn't want to see Johnson get another gold medal."

The daily criticism of Rosen by members of both relay teams was shocking to many of his coaching colleagues. Rosen, trying to stay above the fray, rarely commented to the press, but he quipped to one reporter asking whether the 1600-relay team could successfully run given the dissension: "I don't think it would be helpful for team morale for me to engage in a war of words because our plan is still to put our strongest relay team on the track. They don't have to talk to each other. They just have to pass the baton."[10]

The criticism of Rosen got so bad that F. X. Cretzmeyer, Rosen's coach at Iowa, sent Rosen a fax telling him to hang in there. Rosen: "Did the criticism bother me? Yes, no one wants to be criticized publicly. But it didn't influence any of my decisions about the relays. I did what was best for the team."

The team composition for the 1600-meter relay was made a little less complicated when Everett aggravated an old Achilles' tendon injury and was forced to withdraw from the semifinals of the 400-meters. Because the injury was slow-healing, he wasn't sure he could run in the relay. Rosen decided to replace Everett with Valman. When Rosen told Everett his decision, Everett argued that he could run and should be given a chance. But Rosen wasn't persuaded. "I told Everett that I had someone almost as fast who wasn't injured. It was an easy decision for me. I couldn't take the chance of Everett breaking down during the race. Everett was disappointed but he knew I wasn't going to change my mind." Everett was so angry he wouldn't talk to Rosen for 10 years.

ROSEN ULTIMATELY SELECTED DARNELL Hall, Chris Jenkins, Michael Johnson, and Quincy Watts to run the first round, and Valman, Watts, Johnson, and Steve Lewis to compete in the finals. Rosen wanted Watts, the gold medalist in the open 400, to run second to secure an early lead. Rosen felt Johnson could hold the lead and Steve Lewis would pull away from the field in the anchor position and the team might break the world record.

As Rosen prepared to watch the finals he thought, in spite of all the problems that had revolved around the relay, the team had a chance to break the world record set by the American team in the 1968 Olympics. It was the oldest standing track record. Rosen took out his stopwatch as the teams lined up. At the sound of the gun Valman broke from the blocks and quickly took the lead. He passed the baton to Watts who extended the lead to a remarkable 20 meters. Watts ran his leg in 43.1, the fastest in history, and put the U.S. team under world record time. Rosen had selected Johnson to run third because of his ability to run from the front of the pack. But Johnson, still not completely recovered from a bout of food poisoning, ran a relatively slow 44.8. The U.S. team was now behind world record pace. It was up to Lewis, silver medalist in the 400, to finish the race. "We had such a big lead that it would have been easy for Steve to loose his concentration. I selected him to run anchor because he always ran focused and fast in the lead. He was the perfect runner to finish the race." Lewis extended the lead and powered down the stretch. As he crossed the line, Rosen, like most of the 65,000 fans in the stadium, looked up at the electronic clock. A tremendous roar rose from the crowd as they read the new world record time of 2:56:12.

Rosen: "When we broke the world record all the criticism stopped. All of a sudden I looked a lot smarter to everyone. Winning takes care of a lot of things."

Afterwards, Johnson said, "Everyone was great when it counted. Everyone worked together. Mel Rosen kept saying all summer, 'Everything will come out in the wash.' It did. It did."

ROSEN HAD TOLD HIS staff before competition began in Barcelona that if they won six gold medals, he'd consider it a good meet. If they won seven golds, the meet would be a great success. Should they win eight gold medals, he'd be elected mayor of Barcelona!

The American team dominated, winning eight gold medals. Rosen's goal of placing an American in the finals of every event paid off. The team's 20 total medals were more than any U.S. Olympic team had won since 1960.

As Rosen relaxed in his seat on the long flight home, he thought of Dan O'Brien and Carl Lewis. Had they qualified for their individual events, the American team would have likely won 10 gold medals. But Rosen wasn't disappointed. His experience in Barcelona was everything he hoped it would be. Even the public criticism from the Santa Monica Track Club's athletes didn't sour his Olympic experience. "I'll have good memories of this Olympics." Rosen said soon after the competition ended. "I hate to say, it's like the Army. You don't remember KP duty, but you remember the furloughs."[11]

Rosen also had no second thoughts about retiring from Auburn University. He was ready to move on and looked forward to teaching and assisting new head coach Harvey Glance with Auburn's track team.

He thought about Wilbur Hutsell, the man who had hired him more than four decades earlier. What would his old friend think about his Olympic successes? "I think he'd have been happy for me, but Coach Hutsell was more interested in Auburn's track team. He just wasn't interested in national or international competitions even though he was involved with two Olympics. That is where we differed. I loved the thrill of competing against the world's best."

And his legacy?

"I hope I'm remembered for taking the baton from Coach Hutsell and leading Auburn track to national and international prominence."

Rosen at the Penn Relays sitting next to his friend George Steinbrenner, owner of the New York Yankees, 1999.

'Grandpa, What Do You Know About Running?'

"Everything has worked out well for this little boy from Brooklyn who wound up in the South."

In Rosen's 28-year career at Auburn, he coached seven Olympians, 143 All Americans, 63 Southeastern Conference champions, and eight NCAA champions. He also guided the Auburn University track and field team to four consecutive SEC indoor championships, 1977 to 1980. Furthermore, Auburn won the SEC outdoor conference championship in 1979, a first for the team. Rosen also enjoyed considerable success in international competition, coaching in such places as Japan, Argentina, Italy, and Israel. The pinnacle of his career was coaching the U.S. Olympic track and field team to a record 20 medals in Barcelona.

As a result of his extraordinary achievements, Rosen was recognized by many track and field organizations after he retired from coaching in 1992. He was inducted into the U.S. Track and Field and Cross Country Coaches Association Hall of Fame in 1991, the Alabama Sports Hall of Fame in 1993, the University of Iowa Track and Field Hall of Fame and the U.S. Track and Field Hall of Fame in 1995, and the International Jewish Sports Hall of Fame in 2004. In 2006, Auburn University honored Rosen by naming its new track the Hutsell-Rosen Track.

Why was Rosen so successful? Rosen inspired his athletes. Even though track is an individual sport he taught his athletes to see the importance of the team. Harvey Glance puts it best: "You always wanted to do your best for Mel and not disappoint him. He knew how to make us into a team." That closeness can only develop when athletes feel they are not being exploited and are learning from their coach side-by-side as partners.

Rosen was a great teacher. He calculates that he taught and coached more than 40,000 students during his tenure at Auburn. Most coaches at NCAA Division I schools never see the inside of a classroom. Rosen was an exception. Because he remained in the classroom his entire career, he continually honed his teaching techniques and sharpened his ability to communicate with new generations of students and athletes. Rosen had the remarkable ability to stay relevant without ever compromising his values. He remained "old school" his entire career. Thom Gossom described Rosen as someone who could relate to all athletes, particularly with African Americans. "Mel was a city guy who could relate to us. He had integrity. You always got the sense he cared about you as an individual, not just as an athlete." That is difficult to achieve when athletes and coaches know the only measure of success in big-time athletics is the won-loss record.

IN SEPTEMBER 2009 ROSEN taught his last class. He was 80 years old and had spent 55 years in the classroom. He spoke on the history of track and field. There were about 30 students, some of whom were athletes, the majority not. What struck an observer was how Rosen effortlessly related to students 60 years his junior. Rosen held their attention as he regaled them with sports stories from the past. He has never lost his enthusiasm for the sport he loves, the sport that gave him so much. Red Auerbach said that for Jews growing up in New York City in the 1930s, sports were a ticket to a better life. As a boy in Brooklyn, Rosen understood that and has never forgotten it.

When Rosen took the job in Auburn in 1955, his lifelong friend Sol Saporta chided him about moving to the South. He told him, "'Why do you want to be a Jewish pioneer and go where there are no Jews?' I told him he wouldn't last two years. I guess I was wrong!"

Rosen is one of the few college coaches who spent his entire career at one school. "I never wanted to leave for another job. I know I could have made more money if I had left Auburn, but money has never been what was most important for me." Rosen's salary when he retired as head coach

Rosen and his family at the dedication and renaming of Auburn's track as the Hutsell-Rosen Track in 2007. From left front: daughter Karen, Joan, Mel, granddaughter Chelsy Lami-Payne, and daughter Laurie Lami. Back, grandson Nathaniel Lami and Chris Lami.

in 1992 was $44,000 per year.

Rosen was loyal to Auburn University. He wasn't looking for more lucrative jobs. He always told his recruits that they could count on him to be at the track for them. He delivered on the promise. In the late 1970s, Rosen was recruiting Matt Centrowitz, a distance runner from New York. Despite Rosen's best efforts, Centrowitz accepted a scholarship at the University of Oregon. Centrowitz went on to win the 1980 Olympic trials in the 5,000 meters. Years later Centrowitz saw Rosen at a track meet. He came up to him and said, "Mel, I can't believe you are still at Auburn. When all the other coaches were recruiting me out of high school they said that it would be foolish for me to go to Auburn since you wouldn't last another two years there. They are all gone, and you are still at Auburn!"

THE MEL ROSEN STORY, however, isn't just about his coaching accomplishments, or the awards he's won; it is a story of the Jewish Diaspora. Rosen's story reminds us how Jewish Americans of his generation followed the old Ladino saying, "Every place you go, act according." Simply it says, fit in the best you can. And Rosen and his wife did just that, fit in. Alabama, with its own complex history, provided a place for Rosen and others like him.

However, urgency attends this story. We are reminded that we must listen to those who came before us and celebrate them because they are our link to our past. We must not forget those who paved the way for us. With the advancing years, there are fewer and fewer left of Rosen's generation who came of age in the 1920s and 1930s, who can attest to how far we have all come in our American journey.

As HAS BEEN NOTED throughout this volume, Rosen is able to see the humorous side of things. A story he loves to tell illustrates this point. When his grandson Nathaniel was eight, Rosen went to see him play soccer. He watched as Nathaniel raced up and down the field. Afterwards Rosen took his grandson to the side and explained to him how he could run faster. He showed his grandson how to swing his arms back and forth, how to lean forward, and how to point his toes to gain speed. Nathaniel listed patiently, then as they began to walk to the car, he turned and said, "Grandpa, what do you know about running?"

Because Rosen doesn't take himself too seriously, he understands that good luck has played a significant role in his life. He tried to put that into words when he gave his acceptance speech in Netanya, Israel, when he was inducted into the International Jewish Sports Hall of Fame. "I'll close by saying I can't forget to thank my high school football, basketball, and baseball coaches at Lincoln High for cutting me from their squads so I could go out for track and find my niche in life."

NOTES

PREFACE

1   Ann Lamott, *Bird by Bird: Some Instructions on Writing and Life* (New York: Anchor Books, 1995).

CHAPTER 1: THE PROMISE FULFILLED

1   Irving Howe, *World of Our Fathers: The Journey of the East European Jews to America and the Life They Found and Made* (New York: Harcourt Brace Jovanovich, 1979).

2   Irving Howe and Kenneth Libo, eds., *How We Lived: A Documentary History of Immigrant Jews in America: 1880–1930* (New York: Richard Marek Publishers, 1979).

3   Robert Rockaway, *The Jews of Detroit: From the Beginning, 1762–1914* (Detroit: Wayne State University Press), 111.

4   Zvi Gitelman, *A Century of Ambivalence: The Jews of Russia and the Soviet Union, 1881 to the Present* (Bloomington: Indiana University Press, 2nd edition, 2001).

5   Irving Howe, *World of Our Fathers*.

6   Ibid, 7.

7   John Klier and Shlomo Lambroza, *Pogroms: Anti-Jewish Violence in Modern Russian History* (Cambridge: Cambridge University Press, 1992), 41.

8   Irving Howe, *World of Our Fathers*, 83.

9   Isaac Babel, *You Must Remember Everything: Stories 1915–1937* (New York: Farrar, Straus, and Giroux, 1969).

10   John Klier and Shlomo Lambroza, *Pogroms: Anti-Jewish Violence in Modern Russian History*, 15.

11   Irving Howe, *World of Our Fathers*, 40.

12   Uri Herscher, *Jewish Agricultural Utopias in America, 1880–1910* (Detroit: Wayne State University Press, 1981).

13   Gertrude Wishnick Dubrovsky, *The Land Was Theirs: Jewish Farmers in the Garden State* (Tuscaloosa: The University of Alabama Press, 1992).

14   Ibid.

15   Craig Darch, *Lachiem and Lamentations* (unpublished manuscript).

16   Irving Howe and Kenneth Lebo, eds., *How We Lived: A Documentary History of Immigrant Jews in America*, 197.

17   Henry Feingold, *A Time for Searching: Entering the Mainstream 1920–1945* (Baltimore: The Johns Hopkins University Press, 1992).

18   Jenna Weissman Joselit, *The Wonders of America: Reinventing Jewish Culture, 1880–1950* (New York: Hill & Wang, 1994).

19   Ilana Abramovitch and Sean Galvin, eds., *Jews of Brooklyn* (Hanover: University Press of New England [for] Brandeis University Press, 2002).

20   Nama Sandrow, *Vagabond Stars: A World History of Yiddish Theater* (Syracuse: Syracuse University Press, 1996).

21   Robert Rockaway, "Bad Jews: Jewish Criminals from Brooklyn" in *Jews of Brooklyn* (Brandeis: Brandeis University Press, 1995), 195.

22   Ilana Abramovitch and Sean Galvin, eds., *Jews of Brooklyn*.

23   Ibid.

24   Gerald Sorin, *A Time for Building: The Third Migration 1880–1920* (Baltimore: The Johns Hopkins University Press,1992).

25   Beth Wenger, *New York Jews and the Great Depression: Uncertain Promises* (Syracuse: Syracuse University Press, 1999), 22.

26   Ibid.

27   Bernard Rosenberg and Ernest Goldstein, eds., *Creators and Disturbers: Reminiscences by Jewish Intellectuals of New York* (New York: Columbia University Press, 1982), 289–290.

28   Peter Levine, *Ellis Island to Ebbits Field: Sport and the American Jewish Experience* (New York: Oxford University Press, 1992).

29   Ibid, 96.

30   David Pietrusza, *Rothstein: The Life, Times, and Murder of the Criminal Genius Who Fixed the 1919 World Series* (New York: Carroll & Graf Publishers, 2003), 2.

31   Ibid, 4.

32   Irving Howe, *World of Our Fathers.*

33   Edward Shapiro, "From Participant to Owner: The Role of Jews in Contemporary American Sports" in *Jews and the Sporting Life: Studies in Contemporary Jewry* (Jerusalem: The Hebrew University of Jerusalem, 2010), 90.

34   Robert Slater, *Great Jews in Sports* (Middle Village, New York: Johnathan David Publishers, 1983).

35   Jeffery Gurrock, *Judaism's Encounter with American Sports* (Bloomington: Indiana University Press, 2005), 79.

36   Irving Howe and Kenneth Lebo, *How We Lived: A Documentary History of Immigrant Jews in America,* 72.

37   Stephan Kanfer, *A Summer World: The Attempt to Build a Jewish Eden in the Catskills From the Days in the Ghetto to the Rise and Decline of the Borscht Belt* (New York: Farrar, Straus, and Giroux, 1989).

38   Phil Brown, *Catskill Culture: A Mountain Rat's Memories of the Great Jewish Resort Area* (Philadelphia: Temple University Press, 1998).

Chapter 2: No Looking Back

1   Leah Garrett, "Trains and Train Travel in Modern Yiddish Literature" in *Jewish Social Studies* (7, 2, 2001), 67–88.

2   John Gerber, *A Pictorial History of the University of Iowa* (Iowa City: University of Iowa Press, 1988), 126.

3   *Hawkeye Yearbook* (Iowa City: University of Iowa Press, 1946), 31.

4   Deborah Dash Moore, *To the Golden Cities: Pursuing the American Jewish Dream in Miami and L.A.* (New York: The Free Press, Macmillan Inc., 1994), 1.

5   Edward Shapiro, *A Time for Healing: American Jewry Since World War II* (Baltimore: The Johns Hopkins University Press, 1999), 196.

6   Ibid, 161.

7   Beth Wenger, *New York Jews and the Great Depression* (Syracuse: Syracuse University Press, 1999), 205.

8   Danna Fewell, Gary Phillips, and Yvonne Sherwood, *Representing the Irreparable: The Shoah, the Bible, and the Art of Samuel Bak* (Boston: Pucker Art Publications. Distributed by Syracuse University Press: Syracuse, NY, 2008), 7.

9   Deborah Dash Moore, *To the Golden Cities: Pursuing the American Jewish Dream in Miami and L.A.*, 2.

10   Ibid, 2.

11   Robert Remini, *Short History of the United States* (New York: Harper Collins, 2008), 246.

12   Beth Wenger, *New York Jews and the Great Depression*, 197.

13   Debora Dash Moore, *To the Golden Cities: Pursuing the American Jewish Dream in Miami and L.A.*, 263.

14   Edward Shapiro, *A Time for Healing: American Jewry Since World War II*, 161.

15   Deborah Dash Moore, *To the Golden Cities: Pursuing the American Jewish Dream in Miami and L.A.*, 11.

16   Riv-Ellen Prell, "Triumph, Accommodation, and Resistance: An American Jewish Life From the End of World War II to the Six Day War" in *The Columbia History of Jews and Judaism in America* (New York: Columbia University Press, 2008), 115.

17   Dorothy Schwieder, *Iowa: The Middle Land* (Ames: Iowa State University Press, 1996), 107.

18   Ruth Jacknow Markowitz, *My Daughter the Teacher: Jewish Teachers in the New York City Schools* (New Brunswick: Rutgers University Press, 1993).

19   Marianne Sanua, "Here's to our Fraternity" in *One Hundred Years of Zeta Beta Tau: 1898–1998* (Hanover and London: Brandeis University Press and University Press of New England, 1998), 4.

20   In 1972, Wheeler became head coach of cross-country at the University of Iowa, making him the first black head coach in the Big Ten Conference (Des Moines Register, April 15, 2001).

21   David Halberstam, *The Fifties* (New York: Villard Books, 1993), 289.

Chapter 3: A Plan of His Own

1   Melissa Fay Greene, *The Temple Bombing* (New York: Addison-Wesley Publishing Company, 1996).

2   Ibid, 4.

3   Letter from Wilbur Hutsell to Wilbur Bohm (February 11, 1949), Auburn University Archives (#392 Box 78-4).

4   Letter from Wilbur Hutsell (November 1, 1949), Auburn University Archives (#392 Box 78-5).

5   *Auburn University Track and Field Media Guide*, 2008.

6   Letter from Wilbur Hutsell to James Clark (April 12, 1949), Auburn University Archives (#392 Box 78-5).

7   Letter from Dave Powell to Mel Rosen (May, 14, 1985) (Mel Rosen's Personal Files).

8   Elliott Denman, *Elliott Denman's Anthology of the Olympic Games: Melbourne (1956) to Sydney (2000)* (West Long Branch, New Jersey, 2001).

9   Pete Morgan, "Morgan's Meditations" (*Auburn Plainsman*, January 30, 1963), B1.

10 Letter from James Foy to Mel Rosen (October 4, 1965) (Mel Rosen's Personal Files).

11 Letter from Cretzmeyer to Rosen (November 3, 1963) (Mel Rosen's Personal Files).

12 "Rosen Replaces Auburn's Hutsell" (*The Atlanta Journal*, October, 17, 1963).

13 Richard Wittish, "Rosen-Coach With a One Track Mind" (*Auburn Plainsman*, May, 18, 1967), 8.

14 William Baker, *Jessie Owens: An American Life* (New York: The Free Press, 1986).

15 Ibid.

CHAPTER 4: ONE TRACK MIND

1   Lee Shai Weissback, "Eastern European Immigrants and the Image of Jews in the Small-Town South" in *Dixie Diaspora: An Anthology of Southern Jewish History* (Tuscaloosa: University of Alabama Press, 2006), 133–134.

2   Leonard Dinnerstein and Mary Dale Palsson, eds., *Jews in the South* (Baton Rouge: Louisiana State University Press), 150.

3   Melissa Fay Green, *The Temple Bombing*, 6.

4   Clive Webb, *Fight Against Fear: Southern Jews and Black Civil Rights* (Athens and London: The University of Georgia Press, 2001).

5   Steven Whitfield, *In Search of American Jewish Culture* (Hanover and London: Brandeis University Press and the University Press of New England, 1999), 427.

6   Cheryl Greenberg, "The Southern Jewish Community and the Struggle for Civil Rights" in *African Americans and Jews in the Twentieth Century: Studies in Convergence and Conflict* (Columbia and London: University of Missouri Press, 1998), 123.

7   Eric Goldstein, *The Price of Whiteness: Jews, Race, and American Identity* (Princeton and Oxford: University Press, 2006), 58.

8   Mark Bauman, ed., *Dixie Diaspora: An Anthology of Southern Jewish History* (Tuscaloosa: The University of Alabama Press, 2006), 67.

9   Wayne Flynt, *Alabama in the Twentieth Century* (Tuscaloosa: The University of Alabama Press, 2004), 408.

10 Terry Barr, "Rabbi Grafman and Birmingham's Civil Rights Era" in *The Quiet Voices: Southern Rabbis and Black Civil Rights, 1880s to 1990s* (Tuscaloosa: University of Alabama Press, 1997), 175.

CHAPTER 5: RACE TO THE BOTTOM

1   James Michener, *Sports in America* (New York: Random House, 1976), 255.

2   Letter from Arnsbarger to Rosen (March 26, 1977) (Mel Rosen's Personal Files).

3   Letter from Rowe to Rosen (March 8, 1967) (Mel Rosen's Personal Files).

4   Mel Pulliam, "Mel Rosen Keeps Tiger Track Fortunes at Crest" (*Auburn Plainsman*, May 4, 1966), 8.

5   Larry Lee, "If Mitchell Only Dreamed, No Telling What He'd Do Track-Wise" (*Auburn Plainsman*, May 10, 1964), 8.

6   Letter from Wesley to prospective athlete (February 22, 1971) (Mel Rosen's Personal Files).

7   "SEC Track" (*Atlanta Journal*, March 25, 1964).

8   Tommy Lindsey, "SEC Champion Sprinter Jerry Smith, Another Outstanding Tiger Thin Clad" (*Auburn Plainsman*, May 1, 1963), 7.

9   Gerald Rutberg, "Tiger Topics" (*Auburn Plainsman*, May 6, 1964), 6.

10 Cathye McDonald, "Women Find Track Available on Auburn PE Selection List" (*Auburn Plainsman*, November 27, 1963), 3.

11 Mel Pulliam, "Mel Rosen Keeps Tiger Track Fortunes at Crest" (*Auburn Plainsman*, May 4, 1966), 12.

12 Larry Gierer, "Hair: Players Must Be Well Groomed" (*Auburn Plainsman*, February 10, 1972), 1.

13 Editorial, "Spring is Here!" (*Auburn Plainsman*, March 4, 1971), 30.

14 Editorial, "Athletics Have Important Role in College Says Dr. Philpott" (*Auburn Plainsman*, May 25, 1966), 11.

15 Letter from prospective athlete to Rosen about Auburn's track program (February 26, 1969) (Mel Rosen's Personal Files).

CHAPTER 6: THE BURDEN OF AUBURN HISTORY

1   Martin Olliff, "Just Another Day on the Plains: The Desegregation of Auburn University" (*The Alabama Review*, 2001), 104–144.

2   Jack Bass, *Taming the Storm: The Life and Times of Judge Frank M. Johnson, Jr., and the South's Fight Over Civil Rights* (New York: Doubleday, 1993).

3   Harry Wilkinson, "Integration Policy Stated by Dr. Draughon" (*Auburn Plainsman*, December 4, 1963), 12.

4   Harry Wilkinson, "All is Quiet" (*Auburn Plainsman*, January 8, 1964), 6.

5   Martin Olliff, "Just Another Day on the Plains: The Desegregation of Auburn University."

6   Ibid, 144.

7   Letter from fan to Beard (October 20, 1967), Auburn University Archives (#392 Box 16-10).

8   Letter from Beard to fan (October 24, 1967), Auburn University Archives (#392 Box 16-10).

9   Frank Fitzpatrick, *And the Walls Came Tumbling Down: The Basketball Game That*

Changed American Sports (New York: Simon & Schuster, 1999).

10   Letter from G.W. Beard to Adolf Rupp (March 22, 1966), Auburn University Archives (#392 Box 15-10).

11   Encyclopedia of Alabama (electronic)

12   Letter from Eddie Sears to Jeff Beard (November 5, 1965) (Mel Rosen's Personal Files).

13   Lawrence Epstein, *The Haunted Smile: The Story of Jewish Comedians in America* (New York: Public Affairs, 2001), 227.

14   "Historical New and Notes: Obituary for Robert D. Reid" (*Journal of Southern History*, 46, 1980), 644.

15   John Beck, "Black Athletes Leave Mark on Auburn Sports" (*Auburn Plainsman*, February 13, 1975), 15.

16   Roy Summerford, "Black Athletes Have Broken Race Barriers" (*Auburn Plainsman*, October 3, 1972), 15.

17   Kim Best, "Most Segregated School Appeals Decision" (*Auburn Plainsman,* January 9, 1986), 1.

CHAPTER 7: THE FABULOUS FIVE

1   Roy Summerford, "Black Athletes Leave Mark on Auburn Sports" (*Auburn Plainsman*, March 15, 1983), 22.

2   Roy Bamberger, "Glance Sprinting for Seoul" (*Auburn Plainsman*, April 7, 1986), B 1.

3   Ibid.

4   Richard Hymans, *The United States Olympic Trials for Track and Field 1908–1992* (Indianapolis: USA Track and Field, 1996), 225.

5   Ibid.

CHAPTER 8: NOT QUITE ENOUGH

1   Richard Hymans, *The United States Olympic Trials for Track and Field: 1908–1992*, 245.

2   "Newswire" (*Los Angeles Times*, July 16, 1984), 5.

3   Robert Lindsey, "An Olympic Gold Medal Can be Worth Millions to an American Athlete" (*New York Times*, August 9, 1984), 15.

4   Paul Mayer, *Jews and the Olympic Games: Sport: A Springboard for Minorities* (Portland: Mitchell Vallentine & Company, 2004).

5   Elliott Denman, *Elliott Denman's Anthology of the Olympic Games: Melbourne (1956) to Sydney (2000)* (West Long Branch, New Jersey, 2001).

6   *Notes and Quotes From the Olympics: Press Release for the Los Angeles Olympics*, August 10, 1984.

7   William Taylor, *Anabolic Steroids and the Athlete* (Jefferson, North Carolina: McFarland Publishing Company, 2002).

8   Joseph Turrini, *The End of Amateurism in American Track and Field* (Urbana, Chicago, and Springfield: University of Illinois Press, 2010), 1.

9   Ibid.

10   Nicholas Evan Sarantakes, *Dropping the Torch: Jimmy Carter, the Olympic Boycott, and the Cold War* (Cambridge and New York: Cambridge University Press, 2011).

Chapter 9: Dreams Come True

1   George Wright, *Stan Wright, Track Coach: Forty Years in the Good Old Boys Network* (San Francisco: Pacifica Sports Research Publication, 2005).

2   Joseph Telushkin, *Jewish Literacy: The Most Important Things to Know About the Jewish Religion, Its People, and Its History* (New York: Morrow, 1991).

3   Richard Hymans, *The United States Olympic Trials for Track and Field 1908–1992*, 295.

4   "Rosen Reign to End in Spain" (*Mobile Press*, July 7, 1992).

5   Moore, Kenny. "Images of 1992" (*Sports Illustrated*, December 28, 1992–January 4, 1993).

6   Ibid.

7   Ibid.

8   "Steve Lewis and Everett Take Aim at Coach" (*The Washington Post*, July 29, 1992).

9   Ibid.

10   Julie Cart, "Now Their Silence is Golden" (*Los Angeles Times*, August 9, 1992).

11   Moore, Kenny. "Images of 1992" (*Sports Illustrated*, December 28, 1992–January 4, 1993).

INDEX